This book by Dr. Sau........ ... . only does it convey extremely valuable information to enable pastors and laypeople alike to establish helpful relationships with those experiencing a mental illness; it also demonstrates that it is compassion that drove Martin Luther and should also move us to reach out to those battling spiritual and mental challenges. This book is a gift to the church and all who struggle spiritually and mentally.

Rev. Dr. Daniel Preus,
chairman, Luther Academy

The fall into sin plunged us into holistic unhealth, including struggles with mental health. Yet in His mercy, the Lord gives answer to our need for mental health care. Stephen Saunders tracks the trajectory of sound mental health care from Scripture to Luther to our day. *Martin Luther on Mental Health* splendidly delivers the practical and profound benefit of scriptural teaching and Luther's pastoral care. This gem of a book will be an asset to pastors, deaconesses, and Christians in general, both now and for years to come.

Rev. Dr. Kevin S. Golden, PhD;
associate professor of exegetical theology, Concordia Seminary, St. Louis

Dr. Saunders has offered something for everyone in this delightful new book. Although written to assist pastors, teachers, and laity to better understand and care for those with mental health issues, the book also invites the reader to examine the fascinating intersection between Martin Luther's sixteenth-century theological wisdom and psychology's current cognitive and behavioral strategies for responding to those who suffer. Luther understood life as a time of testing by Satan that would yield affliction, trials, and tribulation. More importantly, he knew that the Christian's suffering seemed to contradict one's certain forgiveness and grace in Christ. Saunders's perceptive discussion of *Anfechtung* and mental illness invites the reader to look anew at the experience of Christian suffering.

The interdisciplinary exploration by Saunders of Tappert's *Luther: Letters of Spiritual Counsel* is supplemented by a useful review and discussion of contemporary diagnoses, cognitive strategies, and behavioral essentials to increase a helper's confidence and effectiveness in conversations responding to individuals struggling with troubling thoughts, behaviors, emotions, and roles. There is no quick and easy GPS available to provide care for others, yet Saunders has provided an array of vital concepts and tools that will be valuable to those who would keep vigil with those who suffer.

Dr. Beverly Yahnke, PhD;
executive director for Christian counsel,
DOXOLOGY: The Lutheran Center for Spiritual Care and Counsel

MARTIN LUTHER ON

Mental Health

Practical Advice
for Christians Today

STEPHEN M. SAUNDERS, PhD

Published by Concordia Publishing House
3558 S. Jefferson Avenue, St. Louis, MO 63118-3968
1-800-325-3040 • cph.org

Manufactured in the United States of America

1   2   3   4   5   6   7   8   9   10   32   31   30   29   28   27   26   25   24   23

Contents

Preface: Why This Book?

In the process of writing *A Christian Guide to Mental Illness*,[1] I came across Theodore Tappert's translations of letters Martin Luther wrote to his friends and family. *Luther: Letters of Spiritual Counsel* was first published in 1955 and has since been republished. Reading the letters Luther wrote astounded me, and I realized then that I had to write this book.

Luther lived and died in the Renaissance. He regularly endured the "physicking" of doctors, who were still trying to figure out how to best apply humoral theory. Luther was both beloved and notorious. The serious disagreements that resulted from his ideas led to orders to kill him on sight. Many wanted him to suffer and rejoiced when they heard he was dead. By his own account, he experienced exhausting and excruciating doubts about his own teaching. But Luther challenged, preached, wrote, and taught because he loved his congregation, his flock. He loved them and wanted them to be assured of their salvation.

These challenges and such a rigorous schedule might convince anyone to yield to despair and exhaustion. To the contrary, Luther never stopped consoling others. He comforted those experiencing spiritual distress and doubt with exhortations about the Bible's inerrant, eternal message of God's great love. Though critical to Luther's ministry, that topic is not the main point of this book.

This book primarily focuses on Luther's kind, compassionate, prescient advice to those experiencing emotional distress. Reading his letters, I was astonished to realize that Luther was dispensing modern mental health advice. He understood and administered counsel that is essentially indistinguishable from what was developed in the twentieth century and used widely today. He focused on the way people think, understood how thinking could cause emotional distress, pointed out how thinking is often incorrect, and advised correct thinking. We now call such counsel cognitive therapy—one of the most effective health care interventions ever developed. In addition, he dispensed advice about behavior. He counseled against isolation and for doing enjoyable things. We now call that behavior therapy—another effective treatment against emotional distress.

This book will not teach you to become a mental health professional, nor will it enable you to do what mental health professionals do. This book must not be taken as encouragement to avoid mental health professionals or to suggest that others avoid them. That would be contrary to what Luther advised. But what Luther wrote to his friends, loved ones, and other souls under his pastoral care remains wonderful counsel to those in emotional distress today. My prayer is that this book provides some guidance to pastors, teachers, and laypersons alike in understanding and helping persons with mental health problems.

Introduction

Mental health problems are common and distressing. They are not new to our age. Everyone knows persons who struggle emotionally. And many persons with mental health problems seek assistance from their church. Perhaps one of the following stories will remind you of a congregation member or a friend. One might even remind you of yourself.

DO YOU RECOGNIZE THESE?

Emily gets very anxious being around others. She attends worship services but leaves quickly after. She has declined invitations to be a Sunday School teacher, to join the choir, and to be on the altar guild. She is shy and often seems depressed, even though she smiles when saying hello. She does not make eye contact readily and always seems eager to leave. During a conversation, Emily discloses to you that she "can't imagine why" others would want her around.

Jerome is a wonderful schoolteacher. You have often thought that he and Emily would be a great couple if either would ever look at the other. He is awkward and prone to depression and seems terribly lonely. You have never heard him mention friends. He gets invited to join other teachers for after-school social gatherings, but he never does. He comes to the Christmas party but leaves early. The principal must constantly reassure him that he is teaching well, especially after a parent makes a complaint or even a suggestion.

Jay is a police officer. He is dedicated to his job, community, and church. He loves his family. He is tall, strong, and has a robust personality. You have known him for years. One afternoon, he pays you a surprise visit and says, "My body aches, my mind aches, and I am bone tired." He says he wants to stop being a police officer—that he is failing his family and is tired of feeling alone in the middle of so many people who rely on him. He wants to leave his job—and maybe leave this life. He says, "Cops do that. It isn't that hard. Maybe Jess and the kids would be better off if I did."

Maggie is very distraught that she spoke unkind words to another church member, a longtime friend. Maggie apologized and was forgiven, but she cannot stop thinking that what she did was unforgivable. She is wondering whether she is—or whether she should be—still welcome at church. This thinking has led her to stop doing things she enjoys. She now attends a different weekly worship service than she has for years. She stopped going to women's midweek Bible study and no longer goes out with church friends. For the first time since you've known Maggie, she looks depressed to you.

Jack has a chronic illness that causes him pain and makes it difficult to get around. Jack does not seem to do much besides work. A software engineer, he has worked from home for over a decade. As far as you know, the only time he gets out of his house is to come to church. Jack confides in you that he is depressed. He attributes it to his medical illness. You wonder if it might also be related to his isolation.

George has a sharp tongue and an acerbic sense of humor. It would be charitable to call his comments witty. Most people simply find him offensive. He is proud of his accomplishments and critical of those who struggle either personally or professionally. People avoid George because his abrasive personality and actions cause hurt feelings.

Barbara is prone to becoming depressed and anxious. She does not know if her faith is, in her words, "strong enough," and she wonders whether she will actually go to heaven. She knows God's promise and can practically recite the catechism from memory, but she ruminates on this concern. She complains that her thinking torments her but says she cannot turn off her mind.

LUTHER KNEW THEM

All of the individuals above are versions of individuals who Luther knew personally. All of them received letters from him that addressed their emotional distress.

Luther and Emily

Emily is based on Elsa Agricola, who was married to Luther's friend John Agricola. Out of concern for how Agricola was doing, being "so fearful and downhearted,"[2] Luther invited her to stay with him and Katie. After Agricola had visited, Luther wrote her husband. Luther rejected anything the physicians and apothecaries, with their "salves of Hippocrates,"[3] could offer. He thought her illness was "more of the soul than of the body."[4] He offered advice about her thinking and her behavior.

Luther and Jerome

Jerome is based on Jerome Weller, the tutor to Luther's children. He lived with Luther's family. He was shy and prone to depression. We have a letter from Luther to him from when Luther was absent from home. Luther wrote that the temptation to yield to emotional distress "is a certain sign that God is propitious and merciful to you."[5] Luther wrote of his own similar experience. He focused on thoughts and behaviors, saying, "Try as hard as you can to despise those thoughts" and, "By all means flee solitude . . . joke and play games with my wife and others."[6]

Luther and Jay

Jay is based on Jonas Von Stockhausen, a captain of mounted knights who policed the town of Nordhausen. The task became burdensome, perhaps related to physical ailments, and he began to experience depression. Luther wrote to be on guard about his thinking: "My dear friend, it is high time that you cease relying on and pursuing your own thoughts." Luther advised, "Listen to other people who are not subject to this temptation."[7]

Luther offered a reassuring perspective, reminding him, "Our Lord Christ also found life to be unpleasant and burdensome, yet he was unwilling to die unless it was His Father's will. . . . Elijah, Jonah, and other prophets likewise found life unendurable, cried out in their agony for death, and even cursed the day on which they were born."[8]

Luther and Maggie

Maggie is based on a woman Luther addressed as "M." Although not certain, it is believed to be Margaret Eschat. What is certain is that the letter's recipient was greatly troubled by words that she had uttered in anger. Luther reminded her that her sin is not greater than God's forgiveness. He stated directly that her thinking was incorrect: "Dear M, you must not believe your own thoughts, nor those of the devil. But believe what we preachers say."[9]

Luther and Jack

Jack is based on Prince Joachim of Anhalt. The prince had a long-standing illness and fever that seemed to cause and be exacerbated by serious depression. The prince's pastor, Nicholas Hausmann, told Luther about the prince, including that he had withdrawn from all the pleasures of the world. Luther would have none of that. He visited the prince and later wrote to him. Luther knew that the prince's behavior was contributing to his depression. He told the prince that it was foolish for a young man like himself to avoid pleasure and cultivate melancholy.[10]

Luther and George

George is based on George Spenlein, a former monk and, at the time of Luther's writing, a cleric. In the spring of 1516, Luther rebuked Spenlein for his sharp tongue and unkind behavior. Cutting right to the point, Luther wrote, "Now I should like to know whether your soul, tired of its own righteousness, is learning to be revived by and to trust in the righteousness of Christ."[11] Luther told Spenlein that his thinking about himself and others was improper. "Cursed is the righteousness of the man who is unwilling to assist others on the ground that they are worse than he is . . . forsaking those whom he ought now to be helping with patience, prayer, and example."[12]

Luther and Barbara

Barbara Lisskirchen, the inspiration for the last story, was the sister of Luther's friends, the Wellers, and was married to George Lisskirchen. The doctrine of predestination troubled her, and the question of whether she was one of the elect tormented her. In counseling her, Luther referred to his own experience with doubt, writing, "I was myself brought to the brink of eternal death by it."[13] He reassured her that doubting thoughts, though distressing and regrettable, were entirely normal. He told her she "must always put these thoughts away from you and turn your attention to God's Commandments"[14] and the assurance of salvation.

LUTHER'S THOROUGHLY MODERN COUNSEL

Luther's ministry to persons in serious psychological distress, such as Elsa, Jerome, Jonas, Margaret, Joachim, George, and Barbara, is documented in the letters he wrote them. We have translations of those letters in Theodore G. Tappert's book *Luther: Letters of Spiritual Counsel.* Similar examples of Luther's words of counsel are written by others, transcribed from what he said at his table.

The letters show that Luther was a warm, caring counselor. Luther always emphasized the reassurance of the Gospel to console those in emotional distress. He knew that the devil was the source of all illnesses, including mental health problems.

But Luther also gave explicit psychological advice that was far ahead of his time. Writing in the sixteenth century, he dispensed mental health counsel developed in the twentieth century. That is the theme of this book.

WHY THIS BOOK?

This book is written to help readers, whether pastor or layperson, do what Luther wrote Matthias Weller in October 1534: "God has commanded men to comfort their brethren, and it is his will that the afflicted should receive such consolation as God's very own. Thus our Lord speaks through Saint Paul, 'Comfort the fainthearted.'"[15]

Pastors know firsthand what research shows. When persons in serious emotional distress seek help, they likely seek it from their church. The reasons for this are understandable. Church is the center of the most meaningful events in people's lives, including the Baptisms of their babies, the catechism and marriage of their children, and the funerals of their parents. The church is where members hear God's message of forgiveness and salvation. The church is where God pours out His gifts of eternal life and salvation in Word and Sacrament. Of course people in emotional distress turn to their church!

Thus this book was written to assist clergy in particular in their duty to care for their church members. But any reader who wants to help people experiencing emotional distress can use the material in this book. As Luther did and as modern mental health professionals do, you can help people in emotional distress change their thinking and their behavior in order to feel less troubled.

BOOK PREVIEW

The first part of this book reviews mental health problems and their treatment. Chapter 1 reviews the rates of mental illness and mental health problems. It shows that they are common. It also documents that most persons in emotional distress do not obtain formal help. There is an intense stigma associated with mental health problems, and that stigma dissuades many people from seeking help. As will be shown, this stigma is exacerbated by the theology of glory, which pervades our society in general and some churches in particular. Chapter 2 provides a guide to understanding what mental health problems are. It shows the association between thinking, behavior, and emotions, which Luther repeatedly wrote about in his letters. Chapter 3 reviews the historical context of Luther's day, especially how illness, including mental illness, was understood and treated. It thus shows that Luther was a man far ahead of his time when it came to understanding mental health problems.

The second part reviews the history of pastoral care and pastoral counseling. Chapter 4 provides a brief history of how pastoral care started to drift from its purpose soon after the Reformation, only to lose its way nearly completely in the late nineteenth and early twentieth centuries. Chapter 4 also suggests that pastors need to emphasize spiritual care more than has become the trend. Chapter 5 emphasizes the importance of spiritual and theological consolation to persons experiencing either *Anfechtung* or mental health problems.

The third part of this book discusses Luther's counsel to those experiencing depression and anxiety as found in his letters, some of his sermons, and what others recorded him saying at his table. I hope to enable pastors and laypersons alike to understand and utilize Luther's powerfully helpful advice. Chapter 6 provides an overview of the impact of thinking and behavior on mental health problems. Chapter 7 then reviews thinking in particular, including what the Bible says about thinking, what mental health professionals know about its effects, and how Luther advised people about their thinking. It ends with specific advice on how to do what Luther did. Chapter 8 does the same for behavior. After reviewing some Bible verses about behavior and then how professionals think about the effects of behavior on mental health, I provide examples from Luther. Then I offer guidance on offering similar advice. In these chapters, I stick as closely as possible to Luther's words and counsel because his counsel is clear, practicable, and useful. I want to be clear; this book will not train readers to be mental health professionals, but it will help readers help people experiencing emotional distress.

The last part of the book addresses other aspects of helping others. I hope to convince readers that they can and should use the advice offered in chapters 7 and 8. But to do so, it will first be necessary to demonstrate that you are listening and that you understand. Chapter 9 discusses some basic issues related to having a helpful conversation with someone in emotional distress. It also reviews other things that churches can do to reach out to persons in emotional distress. It reviews ways to encourage persons to push through the effects of stigma and the depredations of the theology of glory so that they can get the help they need. Chapter 10 wraps things up with an important caveat about helping others. Many people will need professional help. The chapter tries to help readers distinguish between serious problems that must be referred to a mental health professional and less serious issues to which readers can effectively offer assistance. It also provides suggestions for providing a referral when one is needed.

Chapter 1

Rates of Mental Illness and Associated Problems

Do not judge by appearances, but judge with right judgment.
John 7:24

This chapter describes the number of people experiencing mental health problems, including mental illness. It similarly reviews the likelihood of having either of two experiences that create a greater risk of mental illness. The chapter thus shows that everyone knows many persons with mental health problems, troubled histories, or current problems. The cost to individuals and families affected by mental health problems is also discussed. The chapter ends with a discussion of the reasons most persons with mental illness do not seek care despite the variety of effective treatments available.

THE SCIENCE OF EPIDEMIOLOGY

Epidemiology is the study of the prevalence of illnesses in society. Epidemiological studies show, for example, how many people have the flu, cancer, or heart disease, as well as the risk factors for those illnesses. For example, because of epidemiological studies, we know that obesity creates a greater risk of diabetes, heart disease, and other health problems.

How to Count and Report

It is challenging to count the number of persons who have a mental illness. Asking people to self-report will not work, as many will deny out of embarrassment and others simply do not realize they have one. Asking providers how many persons they are treating also does not work since there is no illness—physical or mental—for which all persons seek help.

To study mental illness, researchers go to the homes of randomly selected persons and conduct multihour interviews. They ask about emotions, thinking, and behavior. Interviews comprise over a hundred questions to cover the breadth of mental illnesses. Based on their answers to the questions, the participants are or are not diagnosed with a mental illness, as defined in the *Diagnostic and Statistical Manual of Mental Disorders* (*DSM*).

There are different ways of reporting how many persons in a population have an illness. The most common are annual and lifetime prevalence rates, which define how many persons will experience a mental illness in a given year or in their lifetime.

The Epidemiology of Mental Illness

Since the 1980s, there have been dozens of epidemiological studies of mental illness. The results are consistent across surveys, which reinforces the validity of the results. To summarize, research reveals that mental illness is common and costly. As shown in the table, which summarizes information compiled by the National Institute of Mental Health (NIMH), in the US, not including the substance use disorders (alcohol use or drug use disorders), about one in five adults ages 18–65 will have a mental illness during any given year.

BEST ESTIMATE OF ANNUAL PREVALENCE RATES OF MENTAL ILLNESS[16]	
Any Disorder	21.0%
Any Anxiety Disorder	19.1%
Major Depression	8.4%
Serious Mental Illness	5.6%

Anxiety is by far the most common mental illness, followed by major depression. Mental illnesses vary by severity, and NIMH defines serious mental illness (SMI) as a mental illness that results in serious functional impairment—causing serious limits in one or more major life activities. About one in twenty persons has an SMI in any year. Many persons have more than one disorder. The chance of having a mental illness at some point in adulthood is about 46 percent.[17]

Epidemiological studies of children and adolescents show that mental illness is just as prevalent in them as it is in adults.[18] The disorders that children and adolescents experience, however, are different than those of adults. For example, a common anxiety disorder in children concerns being separated from parents. Children and adolescents have much lower rates of alcohol and drug use disorders, schizophrenia, and bipolar disorder, all of which tend to manifest in adulthood.

RISK FACTORS

By combining epidemiological studies, important information about risk factors for mental illness have been uncovered. For example, men are more likely to develop a substance use disorder, whereas women are more likely to develop depression. Racial and ethnic minorities are more likely to develop a mental illness. Both unpleasant experiences in childhood and being the victim of domestic abuse put a person at a much greater risk of developing a mental illness.

Adverse Childhood Experiences

Abuse and neglect of children are tragically commonplace, and the effects are negative and long-lasting. Since 1998, studies of adverse childhood experiences, or ACEs, have been widely conducted. In a typical study, adults are asked whether they experienced various adverse events in childhood, including physical or sexual abuse, emotional abuse or neglect, or serious family problems (such as parental mental illness or incarceration). Results show that most adults have experienced at least one ACE, and that one in six adults experienced four or more.[19] ACEs predict adult mental health problems, including depression, anxiety, substance use problems, and high-risk behaviors such as smoking and heavy drinking.

Domestic Abuse

Domestic abuse is the experience in adulthood of physical, sexual, and emotional mistreatment by a spouse or partner. Like ACEs, it is common and is associated with mental health problems. A 2010 nationwide, phone-based survey of almost twenty thousand respondents found that about one in three persons reported being the victim of domestic abuse at some point in their lifetime.[20] The consequences of domestic abuse were worse for women, who were much more likely to report psychological ramifications such as depression and anxiety.

Scrutinizing the Numbers

Everybody knows people experiencing mental illness. You might not know who they are, but you know them. If your church has three hundred members, sixty will experience a mental illness in any given year. You can guess that fifty members had four or more ACEs growing up. If two hundred members are adults, sixty-five have experienced some form of domestic abuse.

MENTAL HEALTH, MENTAL HEALTH PROBLEMS, AND MENTAL ILLNESS

Mental health, mental health problems, and mental illness exist on a continuum. At one extreme, there are persons with a diagnosable mental illness. At the other extreme, some persons are fortunate to have consistently good mental health.

In between are persons who experience problems with depression or anxiety but do not meet the criteria for mental illness. For example, to diagnose someone with major depressive disorder, they must have at least five of nine symptoms, such as sadness, insomnia, and low energy. They could have five symptoms, or they could have all nine. But a person who has only four of the nine symptoms does not meet the criteria for depression. Though they do not meet the formal diagnostic criteria of five symptoms, they are clearly in emotional distress. Mental health professionals see many such persons with "subclinical" problems. For our purposes, such persons have a mental health problem, not a mental illness.

The Continuum of Mental Health

A few fortunate people will go through life with uninterrupted mental health, but most persons will experience some level of emotional distress in their lifetime. The illness might come and go without any recognizable cause, or it might emerge during stressful times, such as during cancer treatment or an episode of disabling pain.

Some persons have enduring mental health problems, such as subclinical anxiety, but the problems never develop into diagnosable illnesses. Others have longstanding mental health problems that occasionally worsen into mental illness. Some have a mental illness that never goes away. The term *serious and persistent mental illness*, or SPMI, describes severe versions of lifelong conditions, including schizophrenia, cognitive impairment, and autism. Other mental illnesses are not quite as severe but can last a long time, such as generalized anxiety disorder.

Even within mental health problems and mental illness, there is great variability. There are different severities exhibited by persons with the same mental illness (e.g., depression).

Thus, mental health, mental health problems, and diagnosable mental illness should be thought of as existing on a continuum. In contrast, most persons and most professionals tend to think in categorical terms—in black and white. For them, the person either has a mental illness or they do not.

The Medical Model and Mental Illness

The medical model of illness dominates health care because it tends to work. Its primary supposition is that illness always has an identifiable cause. A body becomes sick because something was inflicted on it (e.g., injury) or infected it (e.g., a virus). The medical model posits that people are either healthy or ill and that if the cause of illness is eliminated, health will be restored. This generally works well in medical situations because most problems indeed have a cause. Someone does or does not have cancer. A heart is or is not damaged. A person got infected by a virus and became sick, but the virus was eliminated, and the person returned to health. An important corollary of the medical model is that treatment should be offered only to those who are definitely ill. Because there is so much variability in mental health problems, because it exists on a continuum, the medical model does not work well.

Consider two examples. Elaine became seriously depressed after her husband drowned during a boating accident. It has been almost two years, and her friends think she should be doing better by now. Should she receive treatment only if she has a diagnosed mental illness? Or might she benefit from talking to a compassionate listener to help her overcome her grief?

Paul is an ex-Marine who saw comrades killed in the last days of the US presence in Afghanistan. Since his discharge, he has had trouble sleeping and often takes medications for recurrent headaches. He does not enjoy going out as much as he did before. Things are much better than when he first returned, but they are not yet back to normal. He does not have a mental illness, but I would argue that he and his wife could use professional help.

Indeed, all persons with mental health problems would benefit from help. The question should not be, "Is this a mental illness?" The proper question is, "Is this problem bad enough to warrant help?"

THE COST OF MENTAL ILLNESS
AND MENTAL HEALTH PROBLEMS

Mental illness and mental health problems cause serious impairment. For example, annual lost economic productivity due to mental illness in the United States is about one trillion dollars.[21] Mental illness is not trivial. It is highly impairing. That said, economic cost is only part of the burden.

Personal Distress Associated with Mental Health Problems

Emotional distress is the defining feature of most mental illnesses, such as depression and anxiety. Persons with mental health problems experience a ceaseless string of distressing thoughts and memories. Perception becomes warped, such that simple interactions can be painful (*For some reason, she clearly dislikes me*). Depression and anxiety create apprehensive anticipation of future events (*If I go to church, people will stare at me*) and can make the person uncertain of even simple decisions.

A less well-known but common consequence of mental illness is physical pain, including headaches and stomach problems. Pain is exacerbated by sleep problems, as anyone with insomnia can tell you, and sleep problems lead to constant exhaustion.

Family Distress

It is proof of God's tender mercy that some persons with mental illnesses, including some with autism, cognitive impairment, dementia, or schizophrenia, escape personal distress because they are unaware of their illness. Anosognosia is personal unawareness of one's illness. Their caregivers, however, are aware.

The family of a person with mental illness suffers the distress of watching a loved one in pain and confusion. They might witness their loved one get insufficient treatment. They might worry when treatment does not work well.

SPMIs, such as schizophrenia and cognitive impairment, can last decades or a lifetime. Some with an SPMI are incapable of caring for themselves, and family members might need to be responsible for the person's well-being. They might feel it necessary to monitor the person carefully to detect warning signs of a relapse in severity. Besides making it difficult to have a full-time job, this caregiving can be physically and emotionally exhausting.

CONCERNING TREATMENT

Treatment for mental illness has advanced tremendously over the last century. The two general categories of treatment are biological and psychological.

Treatment Works

Psychiatric medications affect the biology of the brain. There are medications for schizophrenia, ADHD, bipolar disorder, anxiety disorders, and depressive disorders. They do not usually eliminate a mental illness, but they can significantly reduce symptoms. Psychological interventions have also been developed for most disorders. They involve talking about thoughts and behaviors in order to improve feelings and to improve functioning in roles and relationships. Hundreds of research studies of psychiatric and psychological treatments involving over 150,000 patients and covering nearly all known disorders have been conducted. The findings from these studies reveal that there are effective medications and therapies for almost all disorders. There are specific treatments for particular problems and specially designed treatments for certain populations, such as children and the elderly. It might take time to find the right medications or to connect with a therapist who is a good fit, but if a person with a mental health problem gets care, he or she is likely to benefit.

Most Do Not Seek Treatment

The bad news of the frequency of mental health problems is offset by the good news of treatment effectiveness. Unfortunately, further bad news is that less than half of persons with mental health problems receive treatment. Even worse, fewer than half of those who seek help will be treated by a mental health professional—someone specially trained to diagnose and treat mental illness. Many instead get inadequate care from a provider without expertise.

Treatment Barriers

Persons with mental illness do not obtain appropriate treatment for various reasons. They might be unsure that the problem is serious enough to warrant professional help. They might not know where to obtain treatment, or they might not know what treatment would involve. The most likely barrier to seeking treatment is stigma. Many persons with mental health problems are unwilling to admit that they are suffering and need treatment because our society, and even many in the Christian Church, endorse ignorant and misguided attitudes toward mental health problems.

The next chapter reviews the stigmatizing attitude that many take toward mental health problems, as well as the way Luther understood and comforted those with mental health problems.

Chapter 2

Mental Health, Mental Health Problems, and Mental Illness

Folly is a joy to him who lacks sense,
but a man of understanding walks straight ahead.
Proverbs 15:21

This chapter lays the foundation for how to understand mental health, mental health problems, and mental illness. This modern conceptualization is similar to how Luther thought about these topics. He understood that thoughts and behaviors affect mental health. Luther tried to help people by advising them about their thinking and behavior. We can strive to help our neighbor, as he did, with the knowledge that Luther's advice is consistent with modern psychological science.

THOUGHTS, EMOTIONS, BEHAVIOR, ROLES, AND RELATIONSHIPS

As shown in the figure on the next page, the activities of our minds include thoughts, emotions, and behaviors. These mental activities influence one another. What we think influences how we feel and act. How we act influences our thoughts and emotions. How we feel affects what we do and how we think. These also affect how we do in our roles and relationships.

Emotions (Affect)

Emotions, or feelings, are generally negative or positive. We have a mix of feelings throughout every day. Emotions usually change from moment to moment according to the situation. The intensity of emotions also varies, as seen in the difference between sad and depressed, nervous and terrified, or happy and joyful.

Our emotions are central to our identity, as how we feel about things is perhaps what most defines us. Physically, all persons are nearly identical with similar cells, bones, organs, and biological processes. We differ, however, in whom we like and love, what we dislike and despise. I love my family. You love your family. I like baseball, rock music, and laughter. You like football, country music, and screaming during scary movies.

Our emotions make us who we are.

If you want to make someone feel bad, mock or invalidate their emotions. Tell a child that his or her emotions are silly or stupid, and he or she will feel bad. Thus the essence of love and compassion is to respect and even appreciate another person's emotions.

Affect is a feeling at a particular moment. My affect is happy when I get news of another grandchild on the way, but later my affect is tense during a discussion with a colleague. Mood is an emotion that endures. Mood can be thought of as a baseline emotion or as the way we generally feel.

Affect is emotion from moment to moment, but we usually return to our mood. For example, I was in a really bad mood all day, except when I had lunch with Carol and cheered up for a while.

A mental health professional will evaluate both mood and affect when trying to determine whether someone has a mental health problem. Strongly negative feelings that endure over long periods and do not respond to environmental events, like good news or tense discussions, might indicate a mood disorder. Major depression and bipolar disorder are mood disorders.

Affect that does not change or is inappropriate can be an indication of mental illness. Flat affect is the term to describe the inability to experience emotions. Inappropriate affect occurs when the felt or expressed emotion is incongruent with the situation, like someone laughing at sad news. Major depression is a mood disorder, but it is sometimes called an affective disorder, reflecting that affect does not change but rather stays the same negative tone.

Behavior

Behaviors are actions. Getting up in the morning, showering, brushing your teeth, getting dressed, feeding your children and pushing them out the door to school, getting ready for work, doing work tasks, watching television, listening to the radio, meeting up with friends, talking and interacting with others—these are a small sampling of the behaviors that make up our days. We sometimes act spontaneously, like breaking into song in the middle of the street. Other actions are planned, such as lunch with a friend.

In trying to determine whether a person has a mental health problem, a clinician will evaluate whether a person's behaviors are causing problems. Victor regularly engages in excessive drinking and has problems fulfilling obligations to his family, so Victor will be judged to have an alcohol problem. Amanda rejects invitations to go out with friends because of her depression. Her mood disorder is causing problems in her relationships. Larry is so anxious about flying that he quit his job after earning a promotion that would have required him to travel extensively. His anxiety interfered with his work role. When behaviors cause impairment in roles and relationships, this indicates a mental health problem.

Thinking (Cognitions)

The most important mental activity is thinking. The many ways of thinking are referred to as cognitions. These include memories, assumptions, perceptions, expectations, plans, problem-solving, and so forth.

Cognitions are greatly influential on behaviors, emotions, roles, and relationships. Thinking is required in many behaviors, such as writing or talking. Cognitions, however, also include more automatic activities, such as assumptions about a person or a situation. Our cognitions guide us moment to moment in much of our behavior.

As we think about cognitions, we realize that our minds are essentially timeless. We have memories about the past and think about those memories. Likewise, our thinking is often oriented to the future. We make plans for the future, or we anticipate or expect how something in the future will go.

Given its importance, mental health professionals evaluate a person's thinking in great detail in order to determine whether someone might have a mental health problem. They do this by listening to their stories—listening for how they are thinking—about themselves, other persons, and both past and future events. In particular, they listen for negative thoughts since they essentially determine how someone feels and what someone does, which both affect how well we do in roles and relationships.

Roles and Relationships

Roles define our life's tasks, obligations, and responsibilities. All of us have many roles in life. A parent has many responsibilities, including sustaining children's physical, emotional, and spiritual needs. A husband has a responsibility to his wife to be loving, kind, and faithful. The role of a student entails getting to school on time, going to class, paying attention, and doing homework. The role of an employee is to do his or her job. How well a person fulfills his roles is an important aspect of mental health. A mentally healthy person does not resent, resist, or neglect obligations. She seeks to fulfill them to the best of her ability.

Relationships are what most of us consider to be the most important and rewarding parts of our lives. We may actually define ourselves in terms of our relationships. When asked, "Can you tell me about yourself?" we tell of our families, spouses, and children. We also have relationships with friends, classmates, teammates, and coworkers. Problems in relationships can take many forms. A person with an anxiety problem might avoid others or endure their company with great trepidation. A husband and father with depression might be constantly down, such that his relationship with his wife and children suffers. Spouses who are constantly irritated at each other have marital problems. Problems in developing or maintaining relationships can be due to mental health problems.

Roles and relationships are closely intertwined. Most roles are defined by relationships, like being a spouse, parent, sibling, son or daughter, friend, colleague, boss, or employee. Having a good relationship with your spouse means fulfilling your obligations and responsibilities by making your spouse feel loved, respected, and appreciated.

Mental health professionals evaluate how well a person is doing in roles and relationships to determine whether they might have a mental health problem. Someone having difficulty fulfilling role obligations or forming and maintaining loving relationships might have a mental health problem.

Impairment in either or both might be due to thoughts, behaviors, and feelings.

THE MUTUAL INFLUENCE OF THOUGHTS, BEHAVIORS, AND FEELINGS

Our thoughts, behaviors, and feelings determine one another. Both contemporary mental health professionals and Luther used this notion to counsel people in emotional distress.

Feelings Influence Thinking and Behavior

The way we feel influences how we think. John has a cold and feels lousy. He thinks he will not enjoy a planned lunch with a friend, so he cancels it. Jill thinks baseball is boring and does not care about the game, so she will not watch it. Jay is in constant pain and feels depressed. He thinks he should quit his job. His depression causes him to have difficulty motivating himself to prepare for work, and he is often late.

Behavior Influences Thinking and Feelings

Behavior influences emotions. Someone who spends days without doing something enjoyable will become bored and sad. In contrast, doing healthy, enjoyable things, like going for a walk, having a conversation with a friend, or playing a game, will greatly enhance our emotional state, even if only temporarily.

Our behavior also influences how we think. For example, Juan has acted in a way he regrets. He is unable to stop thinking, *Why did I do that?* By contrast, Andrea has prepared for her upcoming presentation. She thinks to herself, *I'm ready for this!* which makes her feel confident. We have all experienced how our behavior impacts our thoughts and feelings.

Thinking Influences Behavior and Feelings

Our feelings and behavior can greatly influence how we think, but thinking tends to be a greater influence on the other two. The way we think is the predominant determinant of our feelings and behavior.

Thinking and Behavior

The association between thinking and behavior is easy to recognize. We act according to our intentions, decisions, and choices. Even though he has disagreed with her, Michael acts nicely toward Theresa because he thinks she was trying to be helpful. After their disagreement, Lance acts unkindly toward Anne because he thought she was being intentionally uncooperative. Every smoker knows that smoking is unhealthy, but they do not quit because they have decided not to act upon that information. Anthony packs his daughter's school lunch knowing she will eat it later. If you think reading this book is worthwhile, then you are more likely to keep reading it. If I think this car is better than that car, I will purchase accordingly. If you think Jim would make a better president than Joe, your vote will reflect that. Everyone knows how schoolchildren behave if they think a teacher will not follow through on threats of discipline. On the other hand, when students think a teacher will send home a note for misbehavior or missing homework, then they are more likely to behave and do their homework.

There are occasions when an adult's actions cannot be attributed to intention, but these occasions are fortunately rare. Behaviors are a choice. Do not let anyone convince you otherwise. Sometimes anger or sadness gets the better of someone and lead them to do something they should not do. Generally, though, people act how they choose to act, whether they insist that their emotions are to blame or not. When Donald gets angry at his wife, he curses at her. When Donald gets angry after the police officer pulled him over for speeding, he does not curse at him or her. Donald likewise does not curse at his boss, despite being angry about his work schedule. When Donald says to you that he cannot control his anger, do not believe him. He may think that, but it is not true. Behaviors are a choice.

Thinking and Emotion

The association between thinking and emotion is also easily evident. This applies to all thinking, whether past, present, or future-oriented. If I think that I have been mistreated, I will feel angry. If you receive a sympathy card, you will recognize the act of compassion and feel appreciative. Some memories we recall fondly, such as a wonderful vacation, but other memories of unpleasant or even traumatic events are less welcome. Regarding the future, Mary thinks people will mock her singing ability, and she feels anxious about joining the church choir.

Thoughts so thoroughly determine emotions that their distinction is often obfuscated. Thoughts and emotions are casually, regularly, and continually mixed up.

- "I feel like Evan does not like me."
- "I feel that I was treated unfairly by my boss."
- "I feel like I am going to be made fun of when I give the talk."

In each sentence, the word *feel* was used instead of the word *think*. None of the sentences contain an emotion. But it is easily evident how the speaker feels. His or her use of the word *feel* to describe his or her thinking immediately tells us how he or she feels. The sentences clearly indicate that the speaker feels sad, angry, and anxious, respectively. Here are the same sentences distinguishing the thought and the feeling.

- "I *think* Evan does not like me, and that makes me *feel* bad."
- "I *think* I was treated unfairly by my boss, which makes me *feel* upset."
- "I *think* that I am going to be made fun of when I give the talk, and that makes me *feel* very anxious."

Thoughts, Behaviors, and Feelings Impact Roles and Relationships

How a person thinks, feels, and behaves has a large effect on how well he or she does in fulfilling roles and in forming and maintaining relationships. Olivia recognizes that Chris's disruptive behavior is allowed at her workplace, so she finds a job at a different agency. Richard applies for a position but is not hired. He asks for feedback and is told about another position for which he thinks he is more qualified. Because he thinks this, he acts confidently during the second interview and gets the better job. Jon's thinking causes him to skip his sister's Christian wedding out of protest, which hurts her feelings and makes her husband very angry. Though he feels angry, the husband chooses to behave in a manner that expresses support for his wife instead of revealing the full extent of his anger.

The next section discusses how mental health, mental health problems, and mental illness are related to thoughts, behaviors, emotions, roles, and relationships.

Emotions and Thoughts

The distinction between thinking and emotions is extremely important, as it opens up the possibility of helping someone in emotional distress. At the same time, there is much modern misuse of the conflation of thoughts and feelings.

Our feelings are immensely important. They define who we are. I love my family, baseball, and the Beatles. You love your family, basketball, and the Rolling Stones. Our feelings are what make us unique. Anyone who denies our feelings denies the essence of who we are.

This has led to the absurd idea that feelings are always correct. If this were true, how could we help anyone with depression or anxiety? How could we calm someone who is angry? How could we assuage our spouse's hurt feelings? If those feelings were correct, we could not.

Feelings are important and are to be understood, appreciated, and respected. But the modern notion that feelings are always correct has been terribly confusing and outright abused. The reality is that not every hurt feeling is justified. Feelings are based on thinking, and *thoughts can be wrong*. The modern-day hobby of asserting that any hurt feeling is evidence of maltreatment motivated by ill intent is detestable.

Claire is upset because she thinks she was treated rudely by Chris because of her gender. Robert is angry because he thinks that he was not hired because of his accent. Jon hates the Lutheran Church because he thinks it is hateful and hurtful. Their thinking causes them to be upset, angry, and hateful. But Claire is wrong to think Chris singled her out for her gender; Chris is rude to everyone equally. Robert is wrong to think his accent had anything to do with not getting the job offer; he was simply less competent than the other candidates. Jon's hatred is based on scurrilous, tragically commonplace ideas about the Lutheran Church, which are neither hateful nor hurtful.

The absurdity of this modern habit of considering emotions as the ultimate arbiter of facts is quickly revealed in the examples. No one can sincerely claim that feelings always correspond to reality. Many do, though, especially if such an assertion can be used to their advantage or can be used to justify their own hatred. Even though it might not work, we must continue to point to reality, point to facts, and point out errors in thinking. It will not often help, but adhering to the truth in all its forms is all we can do.

DEFINING MENTAL HEALTH, MENTAL HEALTH PROBLEMS, AND MENTAL ILLNESS

We can use the previous discussion about thoughts, behaviors, emotions, roles, and relationships to define mental health, mental health problems, and mental illness.

Mental Health

A mentally healthy person *thinks* accurately and realistically, *feels* much the way he or she wants, and is in control of his or her *actions*. As a result, the person is able to fulfill *roles* and make and keep important *relationships*.

Veronica is in good mental health. She thinks well of herself, knowing she is a sinner, but also knowing God loves her and has redeemed her in Christ. She likewise generally thinks well of others. She generally feels well, with infrequent and temporary feelings of sadness, anxiety, or anger. She is able to do things much the way she wants. She eats well and exercises, does her assigned tasks at work, is pleasant, and treats others with kindness and honesty. As a result of these ways of thinking, feeling, and behaving, Veronica is successfully fulfilling her roles as wife, parent, friend, neighbor, and worker. She has loving and satisfying relationships with the people in her life.

Mental Illness and Mental Health Problems

The *DSM*, published by the American Psychiatric Association, specifies the criteria for various mental illnesses.[22] According to the *DSM*, a person has a mental illness if he or she experiences intense *distress* or exhibits *impairment* in roles and relationships because of problems in *thinking*, *behavior*, and *feeling*.

Most mental illnesses cause profound distress. Indeed, depressive and anxiety disorders are essentially problems of distress. Not all mental illnesses, however, are accompanied by distress. Most people have probably had a friend with an alcohol problem. Drinking does not cause this friend distress, but excess drinking will cause problems in their roles and relationships. The friend shows up late, does poorly on tasks, and makes his wife angry. Hence, a diagnosable drinking problem is not defined by distress but by the problems that the drinking causes.

There are many ways that a person can have problems in thinking, behavior, and emotions, such as a sad mood, unrelenting anxiety, low self-regard, inappropriate guilt, delusional thinking, insomnia, and self-starvation. The many combinations of the three means there are many kinds of mental illness, making the *DSM* quite lengthy.

Changing Thoughts and Behavior to Address Mental Health Problems

The association between thoughts, behaviors, and feelings is the basis of the most common and effective psychotherapy ever developed. Cognitive behavior therapy focuses on changing cognitions and behaviors so that the person feels better and does better in his or her roles and relationships. As we will see, Luther advised cognitive behavior interventions five hundred years before we called it that.

STIGMATIZING THOUGHTS, EMOTIONS, AND BEHAVIOR

As noted in the previous chapter, in any given year, one in five persons will be diagnosed with a mental illness. Over the course of a lifetime, about one in two persons will experience one.[23] Fortunately, there are many effective treatments for all illnesses. Unfortunately, most persons with mental health problems do not seek treatment for them.[24] They are reluctant to tell their doctor, family, pastor, coworkers, or friends. Since they do not tell anyone what they are experiencing, it is impossible to help them.

They are often reluctant to acknowledge emotional distress because of the stigma society holds toward mental health problems.[25] Understanding and addressing stigmatizing thoughts toward mental health problems is the first step in being able to help.

Stigmatizing Thinking Leads to Negative Emotions and Hurtful Behavior

Society has very particular and derogatory ideas about mental illness. A common belief is that persons with mental illness are dangerous and unpredictable. These thoughts lead to feelings of fear and the behavior of avoidance. Another idea is that a person with mental illness must deserve it; it must be a punishment or the result of something bad that they did. Some people believe that mental health problems happen only to the weak. Strong people "fight through it" and "tough it out." These thoughts lead to pity and scorn, not to mention unkind behavior. We might help an elderly person who struggles to stand. We acknowledge that age and frailty are not their fault. By contrast, we often stigmatize those with mental health problems as bad or weak persons who do not deserve help.

It is likewise unfortunately common to think that parents and families are to blame for mental illness in children. As seen in the first chapter, if a child is abused, he or she are much more likely to have a mental health problem as an adult. To blame all emotional issues on parents, however, is problematic and unfair. Freud never said that parents were to blame for their child's mental illness. If someone thinks parents are to blame when a child has a mental illness, he may feel anger toward those parents. If he witnesses parents struggle with a child with serious mental illness, he will likely not offer help, nor a kind word, nor even a prayer.

Make no mistake, persons who struggle with mental health problems and their families know very well how some view them. They know that some look down on them with scorn, pity, fear, and revulsion. They have had these ideas stated directly to them. They may have actually had their pastors communicate this to them, whether explicitly or subtly.

Stigma Interferes with Getting Help

The result of these stigmatizing attitudes is predictable. Persons with mental illness tend to feel unworthy of love and unwelcome in society.

Thus, a person with mental illness will almost inevitably also develop a sense of isolation, shame, and embarrassment.

If you were them, you would do what they do: keep your suffering to yourself. If you anticipated hurtful reactions, you, too, would say nothing to provoke them. Persons suffering the effects of mental health problems, either personally or with a loved one, tend not to talk about their struggles. It is bad enough to suffer, and they don't want to add embarrassment. Need proof? Of the people you know, how many can you identify as having a mental illness? How many have spoken openly about it?

Since they think they are unable to talk about their mental health problem, they will not hear that mental illness is common and treatable. They will not be encouraged to seek help. They will not obtain help from you or a professional. In a similarly tragic manner, many families insist that their child not obtain help for a mental health problem because it would embarrass the family.

I hope this book helps readers understand and address the widespread stigma our society, and some in the church, hold toward mental illness and mental health problems. I hope to show readers how Luther rejected such attitudes and instead offered compassionate, loving, empathic, and sympathetic comfort and consolation, as well as really good advice. Luther recognized, as should you, that Christians may have an additional burden of stigma.

The Devastation of the Theology of Glory

Christians may think—or worry that others think—that mental health problems are due to sin, lack of faith, or punishment from God. These things are scurrilous falsehoods and outright heresies, but theologians of glory and their many followers believe and preach exactly this. It is easy to fall into the trap of worrying about these things. Know that persons in your church do not hear the theology of glory at your church, but they nonetheless hear it every day.

In this way, a Christian who suffers from a mental health problem simultaneously with the depredations of the theology of glory is in grave danger (I will dig more into the theology of glory in later chapters). He or she needs to hear God's words of love. He or she needs the embrace of the community of believers.

You and your church can offer comfort and consolation to those with mental illness and their loved ones. The church does not flinch from sickness and sorrow. The church does not attribute suffering to weakness and to sin (except original sin, which led to the fall of the entire world). The Church preaches Christ crucified for all.

In the chapters to come, we will note that Luther began essentially every letter of consolation to persons experiencing emotional distress with an assurance that their struggles were not deserved. In the next chapter, Luther's remarkable insights and compassionate responses are placed into his personal history and into the context of the medical field in his time.

Chapter 3

The Medico-Historical Context of Luther's Advice

Jesus Christ is the same yesterday and today and forever.
Hebrews 13:8

This chapter gives an overview of the historical context of Luther, including medical care of the time. We will see the enduring dominance of the humoral model of health, Luther's personal familiarity with physicians, and his very practical advice regarding medicine and health. A review of Luther's own physical and emotional struggles underscores and helps explain his striking insights into persons in emotional distress.

THE RENAISSANCE ERA

Luther (1483–1546) lived during the Renaissance. Humanistic scholars of the late fifteenth century insisted on distinguishing the Renaissance era from the so-called Middle Ages or Dark Ages, a pejorative term they invented to describe the previous thousand years or so when civilization fell into "darkness." This was due to the downfall of the Roman Empire and the pervasive, although not complete, loss of Greek and Roman scholarship. The rediscovery of these classical works led to increased scholarly activity in science, art, politics, architecture, and medicine. These, in turn, eventually culminated in the Renaissance or "rebirth."

Despite the protestations of the scholars of the era, however, the Renaissance was still medieval in many ways. The decline of the feudal system exacerbated rather than addressed social unrest, as evinced by the many peasant uprisings. Warfare continued, and disease was rampant. The bubonic plague reached its apex decades earlier, but it regularly reappeared, as Luther often noted in his letters. Medicine advanced, but truly effective treatments for ailments were rare. For most diseases, either the body recovered or it did not, regardless of the ministrations of physicians.

For persons with mental illness, it was probably a particularly difficult time. On top of the terrible stress, which both triggers and intensifies mental illness, there was an almost complete lack of ability to help. The only thing available to those with mental health problems were kind words and practical assistance with the tasks of living. Those with serious mental illness had it very bad. Though serious *medical* illness tended to end in either recovery or death, persons with serious *mental* illness neither recovered nor died. They simply stayed sick and relied on others for care, which at best meant confinement in the home or, considerably worse, confinement in a mental asylum.

A 1484 papal decree that clergy should strive to identify and exterminate witches probably did not help attitudes toward mental illness. To aid this mission, two German Catholic priests wrote *Malleus Maleficarum (Hammer of Witches)* in 1486. Thanks to Gutenberg's press, it was widely read for the next two centuries. It described methods for identifying witches. It was believed that witches were primarily women, as they were more vulnerable to the devil's wiles. Witches might have moles or insensate spots on the body, presumably created when the devil entered the person. They might have a disheveled appearance and talk to themselves, both commonplace in persons with serious mental illness. Thus it is believed that some persons with serious mental illness were caught up in the frenzy of witch hunts.

That Luther believed in witches is evident in his 1518 sermons on the Ten Commandments. He certainly believed in the real presence of the devil. He never stopped talking about the assaults of the evil one. In one of the last letters he wrote his wife, Katie, perhaps somewhat tongue-in-cheek, "The devil has spoiled the beer everywhere with pitch, and he spoils your wine at home with sulphur."[26] Luther referred to angry outbursts, fears, depression, and physical ailments as assaults of the devil.[27]

More than many of his time, though, Luther had understanding and compassion toward those with mental health problems. His attitude was all the more astonishing given what was known about illness and its treatment during his era. Such knowledge relied primarily on the teachings of a physician who lived 1,200 years prior.

MEDICAL CARE IN LUTHER'S TIME

Explanations for the cause of ill health have changed greatly over the centuries. One thing has never changed, however: the presumed or proven cause inexorably leads to the attempted treatment. For example, some believed mental illness was caused by evil spirits trapped in one's skull. "Treatment," therefore, entailed *trephination*, which was the drilling of a hole in the skull to allow spirits to escape.

Notions about both cause and treatment during Luther's era of illness were based on the teachings of a physician who had lived 1,500 years earlier. Galen of Pergamon (129–ca. 216 BCE) borrowed ideas from Hippocrates (ca .460–ca. 375 BCE), the Greek physician who died over five centuries before Galen was born. We justifiably admire the enduring influence of Hippocrates. He is referred to as the father of medicine and is immortalized in the oath that bears his name in which medical students swear to be ethical. Galen's influence, though, was much greater and has endured much longer.

The Humors of Hippocrates

Humoral theory likely started in Egypt, but it is ascribed mostly to

Hippocrates. In a work often attributed to him, *On the Nature of Man*, he wrote that the human body contained four humors, blood, phlegm, yellow bile, and black bile. Health existed when the humors were in the correct proportion to one another, whereas illness and pain resulted when one of the humors was out of balance.

Hippocrates was a great and admired physician, but many scholars think that much that is attributed to him was actually produced by his admirers. Attributing their own ideas to him or claiming that Hippocrates wrote what they actually authored would strengthen the legitimacy of their ideas, claims, and writings. In contrast, we have lots of work directly from Galen.

The Teachings of Galen

Born in what is now Turkey, Galen studied medicine in Egypt. He began his career in Pergamon, which had a library second only to the renowned library in Alexandria. He worked for three years as a surgeon at a school for gladiators, which undoubtedly helped his understanding of injury and the human body.

After moving to Rome, Galen gained a reputation for compassionate care. According to scholarship,[28] he was a dedicated physician who spent hours and days with his patients. He bathed, massaged, cooked for, and fed them. His renown was enhanced by public demonstrations of his ministrations to the sick, as well as animal dissections. He applied what he could learn from these animals to what he could observe about the human body, such as the importance of body temperature and heart rate. His fame was such that his patients included Roman emperors. His enduring influence, however, had other causes.

Perhaps the best explanation for the colossal influence of Galen is that, in contrast to Hippocrates, we definitely have many writings of Galen. Several hundred works are attributed to him, and over a hundred of those works survive to this day. He reportedly had twenty scribes write down his every observation. His writings circulated widely. Though basically lost for centuries in medieval Europe, they were translated and preserved by Arabic scholars. When they were brought back to Europe, they were incorporated into medical university teachings and texts and became a huge influence in the Renaissance.

Not only did he write prolifically, the quality of his study of the human body was completely unprecedented. Galen's description of the human body was very detailed, which lent authority to his work. Foreshadowing the scientific revolution centuries in the future, Galen offered evidence others could replicate or repudiate. He made astute guesses about the nervous and vascular systems. Later, proof bolstered his influence. Centuries later, his writings gained the approval of the Catholic Church, in part because he was a monotheist—referring constantly in his writings to "the Creator"—and he incorporated religious ideas into his writings.

The Dominance of Galen's Humoral Treatments

Hippocrates was influential in medicine, but Galen was ascendant. His ideas directed medical thinking, teachings, and practices for 1,500 years. Galen agreed that if the four humors (or fundamental fluids in the body) are somehow out of equilibrium, then disease results. Cause then directs treatment.

To restore a proper balance of humors, Galen had patients ingest herbs and potions that had purgative (laxative) and emetic (nausea and vomiting) effects. Thus the emergence of the apothecary can be attributed to Galen. Apothecaries (equivalent to modern pharmacies) mixed herbs, metals, minerals, animal fat and blood, and maybe even a bit of earwax to create potions and lotions to "treat" illness.

Blood was one of the four humors, and Galen practiced and adamantly defended the practice of bloodletting in order to get it into better balance. The "treatment" endured longer than the use of purgatives and emetics. This is somewhat puzzling, given that bloodletting causes such obvious negative effects. Consider, though, that the immediate effect was the weakening of patients, often followed by sleep. Sleep is beneficial to the ill and much preferred to the struggle with pain or coughing fits. It was not until clear scientific evidence against the practice became widely accepted that bloodletting started to lose favor.

The influence of humoral theory, as promoted by Galen, is still seen today. For example, think about persistent emotional states. Almost two millennia after Galen, we describe the angry, easily-irritated as choleric (*kholera* was yellow bile). The unemotional person is phlegmatic. *Sanguineus* is Latin for "of blood," and the sanguine person is well-regarded for being cheerful and optimistic. And, of course, *melankolia* (black bile) is the term in Luther's day, and a term still sometimes used, to describe depression.

Galen's ideas about the cause and treatment of illness were extremely influential during Luther's time. We will see that Luther had much personal experience with them.

LUTHER AND PHYSICKING

Luther recommended physicians. He did not always like what they did to him, but he was clear that God had provided them for our benefit. Luther was quite familiar with both physicians and their ministrations.

Luther Promoted Medicine and Science

Luther said repeatedly and vehemently that illness, including mental illness, was the work of Satan, the prince of death. But Luther recognized the importance of physicians. In one of his Table Talks, he is recorded as saying about medical care,

> "Physic has not its descent and origin out of books; God revealed it. . . . Therefore we may justly use corporal physic, as God's creature." More explicitly ridiculing the idea that

only God's direct intervention should be relied upon, Luther continued, "Our burgomaster here at Wittenberg lately asked me, if it were against God's will to use physic? For, said he, Doctor Carlstad has preached, that whoso falls sick, shall use no physic, but commit his case to God, praying that His will be done. I asked him: Did he eat when he was hungry? He answered, yes. Then, said I, even so you may use physic, which is God's creature, as well as meat and drink, or whatever else we use for the preservation of life."[29]

Luther advised practical steps that were consistent with scientific knowledge at the time. Regarding the plague, for example, Luther believed in using every reasonable precaution. "Use medicine. Take whatever may be helpful to you. Fumigate your house, yard, and street. Avoid persons and places where you are not needed or where your neighbor has recovered."[30]

Luther recommended these things even though he knew that the fallen world and the devil, in particular, was the source of all illness, including mental illness. He said, "In cases of melancholy and sickness, I conclude it is merely the work of the devil. For God makes us not melancholy, nor affrights nor kills us, for he is a God of the living."[31]

Luther's Own Illnesses

We know much about the medical afflictions that Luther suffered because he wrote about them often and openly in his letters. Luther was not stoical about his ailments, but neither should we call him a hypochondriac. As Tappert writes in an understated fashion, "Sickness played a large part in the lives of people in the sixteenth century."[32] Luther's letters reference medical ailments that both he and his correspondents would have experienced.

Luther thus had much personal familiarity with medical practitioners. His particular afflictions were generally well-known to physicians of the time. They knew what he was suffering, such that Luther was able to relate to his correspondents his maladies. Luther wanted them to pray for him.

From Wartburg, in May 1521, Luther wrote Melanchthon, "The Lord has visited me with great bodily suffering. I have not slept all night, and had no rest. Pray for me."[33] He wrote a letter in 1537 to his wife, Katie, and mentioned the passing of a kidney stone: "The earnest prayers of so many people have effected what medicine was powerless to do, and last night I got relief, and feel as if I has been born anew."[34]

Among the illnesses Luther experienced, pain was the common result. He experienced stomach pain; severe chest pain (*angina pectoris*) due to high blood pressure; gout; chronic constipation; bleeding hemorrhoids; kidney stones and bladder stones; and a chronic, decade-long open sore or ulcer on his left leg.

Over the last two decades of his life, he was afflicted with what researchers now believe could have been Meniere's disease, a disorder of the inner ear that causes tinnitus and dizzy spells. He described his symptoms to Melanchthon on May 12, 1530, saying about his experience at Schmalcalden, "I felt a loud buzzing and roaring, like thunder, in my head, and had I not stopped at once I would have fainted, and was useless for two days."[35] The illness caused him severe headaches, and he often had to avoid bright sunlight. Given this, it is comical to read that Luther had a "tendency" toward emotional outbursts and irritability. Who would not be cranky if afflicted with such painful illnesses?

Given his illnesses, Luther often endured the ministrations of physicians. Luther had a love-hate relationship with them. In the same letter to Melanchthon, he attributes his improvement to their ministrations: "The noise in my head is subsiding through medicine."[36] In a previous letter acknowledging that physicians were essential, he wrote Melanchthon on July 13, 1521, "If I do not improve I shall go to Erfurt and consult the physicians, for I can endure my malady no longer."[37] At the same time, he often disparaged or at least teased physicians in clear reference to their reliance on the ideas of Galen. At the table, Luther said about his illness,

> When I was ill at Schmalcalden, the physicians made me take as much medicine as though I had been a great bull. Alack for him that depends upon the aid of physic. I do not deny that medicine is a gift of God, nor do I refuse to acknowledge science in the skill of many physicians; but, take the best of them, how far are they from perfection?

Luther knew why they were doing this, but he was also skeptical. In the same talk, Luther goes on to report that the doctors were "acting upon certain theories, but, at the same time, they must not expect us to be the slaves of their fancies. We find Avicenna and Galen, living in other times and in other countries, prescribing wholly different remedies for the same disorders. I won't pin my faith to any of them, ancient or modern." [38]

LUTHER'S MENTAL HEALTH

Luther openly acknowledged struggles with emotional turmoil, including that he experienced depression. Luther wrote Jerome Weller, who was experiencing his own depression, in July 1530, "Let me remind you what happened to me when I was about your age. When I first entered the monastery it came to pass that I was sad and downcast, nor could I lay aside my melancholy."[39] He stated to Prince Joachim in a letter dated May 23, 1534, that he struggled with depression much of his adult life: "I myself, who have spent a good part of my life in sorrow and gloom."[40] Luther acknowledged that he was prone to fits of anger, but he noted that anger helped him when confronting enemies, writing, and preaching.

Even without such direct admission, we can witness some of his emotional distress in his letters to his wife and to his friend Philip Melanchthon. On June 11, 1530, he wrote complainingly, even petulantly, to Melanchthon, "I now see that you have all entered into a compact to torture us by your silence. But I herewith announce that we shall now vie with you in your silence, although possibly that will not disturb you. I must praise the

Wittenberg people, who, although as busy as you, have written thrice before you sluggards wrote once." He ended with, "I lay down the pen, so that my constant writing may not drive you into a more persistent silence."[41]

Physical and Mental Health

Much of Luther's emotional turmoil can be attributed to his severe physical ailments, which were both chronic and painful and worsened with age. He knew this himself, writing a friend, "Our physical health depends in large measure on the thoughts of our minds. This is in accord with the saying, 'Good cheer is half the battle.'"[42] Any reader who has experienced serious depression understands that emotional turmoil is felt throughout the entire body, not just in the mind. Conversely, any reader who has experienced chronic pain knows it is debilitating to mental health.

An oft-quoted letter presented as evidence of Luther experiencing depression actually strongly suggests that his emotional turmoil was due to physical illness. He wrote Melanchthon in early August 1527, "For the last week I have been thrown into hell and the pit, my whole body so bruised that I still tremble in all my members. I had almost lost Christ and was thrown to the billows and buffeted by storms of despair so that I was tempted to blaspheme against God."[43] This is quoted to document that Luther experienced depression. Luther, though, was in extreme physical discomfort and truly believed he was dying, as evinced by first-hand testimony, including his own. Working backward in time, on July 10, 1527, Luther wrote Spalatin, who was in ill health, "Three days ago I, too, was seized with a sudden attack of weakness, so that I despaired of life and thought myself about to die before the eyes of my wife and friends."[44] Three days later yet, he wrote Nicholas Hausman that he was still "suffering from a severe prostration."[45]

One of the friends Luther feared he was dying in front of was Justus Jonas, who wrote from Wittenberg on July 7, 1527, to document the sudden illness that had afflicted Luther. He wrote that he and his wife had been invited to the Luther's home for supper that day. During supper, Luther "complained of a loud and troublesome roaring in the left ear, which the physicians said was a precursor of a fainting spell." He prayed and asked those around him, including Katie, to be steadfast should he die. Jonas wrote, "Then he sobbed and shed copious tears."[46] Luther also asked to see and said goodbye to his son Hans.

Physical torments assailed Luther and affected his mental health. Luther used these experiences to advise others. But Luther also had personal experience with other causes of mental health problems, and he used these experiences in his advice as well.

Luther's Experience with Isolation

After the pope determined to kill Luther, he was secreted and sequestered to the isolated fortress of Wartburg. Over time, perhaps because of growing depression, Luther isolated himself from the others at the fortress. A while later, he succumbed to depression. He wrote Melanchthon on July 13, 1521, "Instead of being ardent in spirit I am the prey of sinful appetites—laziness and love of sleep. For eight days I have neither prayed nor studied, through fleshly temptations."[47] In the same letter, Luther complained, presumably in bitter jest, that his depression was his friend's fault: "When things are going so well with you I am not needed."

Later we will see that Luther recognized that his own behavior made his depression worse. Thus Luther, from his own experience, cautions others in emotional distress against isolating themselves.

Anfechtung and Mental Illness

Regarding his own emotional turmoil, Luther primarily spoke of *Anfechtung*, the inevitable torments associated with being a Christian and suffering doubt. Luther's physical and emotional suffering sometimes drove him to despair of God's love for him.

Because they are so closely connected, many authors make a mistake in not distinguishing Luther's mental health problems from his *Anfechtung*. But they are distinct, in him and in us. In the same way that physical and mental health are mutually influenced, contributing to each other, *Anfechtung* and mental health problems greatly influence each other. They are not the same, though. In his correspondence, Luther recognized this. This is further explored in chapter 5.

SUMMARY: LUTHER'S EXPERIENCES AND LUTHER'S COMPASSION

Some foolishly arrogant psychologists, such as Erik Erikson, and some arrogantly foolish Roman Catholics, such as Peter M. J. Stravinskas, have attempted to attribute Luther's theological perspective to mental health problems. Suffice it to say that if one rejects the notion of God (as does Erikson) or rejects the idea that a reformation of the church was necessary (as does Stravinskas), then one needs an alternative explanation to Luther's profound and lasting importance to the Christian faith.

In contrast to such folly, we can appreciate how Luther's personal and extensive experience with physical health problems, mental health problems, and *Anfechtung*, in combination with his profound intelligence, remarkable compassion, and intense desire to help others, gave him great insight into what others in distress needed. Particularly astute were his insights into human psychological functioning. I will argue that his psychological insights closely paralleled his theological insights. In other words, Luther's theology was his psychology. In both, Luther emphasized proper thinking and understanding.

Chapter 4

Return Pastoral Care to Its Proper Place

*Beware of false prophets, who come to you in
sheep's clothing but inwardly are ravenous wolves.*
Matthew 7:15

This chapter reviews how pastoral counseling lost its way
from a focus on salvation to a focus on self-esteem. It
reiterates what better writers and actual theologians have
said, which is that the proper task in pastor care is to focus on
Christ crucified.

PASTORAL CARE BECAME PASTORAL COUNSELING

In his masterly and thorough history, E. Brooks Holifield documents how pastoral care devolved into pastoral counseling. The work of the pastor changed from a focus on salvation to a concern about self-realization.

Lutheran Pietists Seek to "Complete" the Reformation

Some Lutherans considered the Reformation incomplete because it did not adequately resolve the torment of *Anfechtung*—doubts about one's salvation. Calvin's preaching of predestination exacerbated this issue, as many worried there was nothing they could do either to assure or destroy their salvation. Indeed, Luther wrote numerous letters to persons tormented by this theological construct.

Lutheran Pietists of the seventeenth century taught that believers should not just know they are sinners. They should feel it. Those who did not were described as spiritually "dry" or "dead." But they also wanted believers to experience the good feeling of being truly repentant.

Thus, eighteenth- and nineteenth century treatises on how to act like a pastor emphasized the ability to understand human nature. In about the same era, between 1600 and 1800, the two concepts began to merge. What once meant *to save the soul* now meant *to transform the mind*. So treatises of the time asserted that the pastor needed to become an expert in the mind. The pastor needed to be someone who could analyze motives, evaluate feelings, and uncover hidden intentions. Pastoral care slowly transformed into an effort to eliminate sin by helping parishioners gain control over sinful thoughts, feelings, and behaviors.[48]

This way of thinking—that the mind is the soul and that salvation is to be both earned and felt—was nothing new, of course. But its dominance in the United States, in particular, cannot be exaggerated. Holifield[49] shows how this groundwork, established largely by Lutheran pietism, contributed greatly to America's intense and near-immediate embrace of the developing science of psychology.

Then Came Psychology

Helping parishioners better control their thoughts, motives, feelings, and behaviors so that they could avoid sin and feel more assured of their salvation required an understanding of their inner state. Fortunately, the field of psychology was developing at about the same time, and it explicitly explored the workings of the mind. Thus, pastors who were influenced by this notion were hopeful that they could learn from psychology to guide the minds of their parishioners away from sin.

The transformation from pastoral care to pastoral counseling became unambiguous in the early twentieth century. The Emmanuel Movement[50] began in an Episcopal church in Boston, and it explicitly blended the ideas of psychotherapy and religion. The importance of mental health professions became incontrovertible after the two world wars, as the wars focused attention on the undeniable psychological needs of millions of traumatized persons around the world.

Not coincidentally, the formalization of how to understand and treat psychological problems by Sigmund Freud (1856–1939) became practically universally accepted. Most importantly, he gave a detailed explanation of the cause of mental health problems and directives on how to address them. Although his ideas about problems being due to unconscious forces were neither new nor revolutionary, over time, they have become associated with him because he wrote eloquently in a style that both academics and the general public could appreciate. That said, Freud's ideas about treatment were indeed revolutionary. That mental illness could be cured gave thousands of doctors who had no real means to help—and the millions of persons and their families in distress—something to which they could turn.

The professionalization of pastoral counseling soon followed. This was in part because pastors now faced challenges from other professions—neurology, psychiatry, psychology, and social work—that also were dedicated to the alleviation of emotional distress.[51] The term *pastoral care* was replaced with *pastoral counseling* to sound more professional and to fit within the field of counseling. Pastoral counselors were thus able to find positions in hospitals, prisons, schools, and mental health clinics. In the 1930s, clinical pastoral education became a regular part of many seminaries' curricula.

The ideas of another highly influential mental health professional, Carl Rogers (1902–87), became even more widely accepted with pastoral counseling. His notion of unconditional positive regard resonated with pastoral theologians. Also, the notion of self-realization appealed greatly to pastoral counselors interested in helping others become better people, justifying their salvation, and calming their spiritual distress. If the counselor can help the person remove unhealthy inner habits of thinking, the person can actualize into the best person they can become, engaging in acts of care, concern, and generosity toward others.

By the late twentieth century, pastoral care lost its way. Pastoral care had become pastoral counseling, which was literally meant as another term for "mental health counseling." Preaching Christ crucified became less important than helping people undermine their sinful behavior, become self-assured of their salvation, and calm their anxious souls. Instead of pointing the way to salvation, today's pastoral training tends to focus on the pastor's role as a companion on one's spiritual journey rather than as a caretaker of souls. In short, it happened because the essential teaching of the theology of glory never loses its appeal: if you feel good about yourself, God must surely look upon you and be pleased. A focus on salvation gave way to a focus on psychological phenomenon. Initially intended as a way to help parishioners overcome their sinful nature, over the decades, pastoral care has increasingly attempted to mimic secular counseling and help persons in emotional distress.

This book attempts to show how Luther's insight into mental health problems was prescient and is very similar to modern mental health care. In subsequent chapters, I will show that his ideas can be utilized today by pastors and laypersons alike to help persons in emotional distress. Doing so is part of *Seelsorge*, or the care of souls. Luther emphasized repeatedly that the main concern and the primary duty of pastoral care is to address spiritual needs. The next chapter, therefore, tries to distinguish spiritual needs, *Anfechtung*, and emotional needs to help return pastoral care to its proper place.

Chapter 5

Anfechtung and Mental Illness

Trust in the LORD with all your heart, and do not lean on your own understanding. In all your ways acknowledge Him, and He will make straight your paths. Proverbs 3:5-6

This chapter reviews the distinctions and similarities between spiritual distress and mental illness, as well as how they influence each other. I also provide brief advice on the importance of addressing spiritual distress in every Christian, and especially those in emotional distress.

DISTINGUISHING *ANFECHTUNG* AND MENTAL ILLNESS

In a letter to Melanchthon dated May 26, 1521, Luther stated, "Do not be anxious about me, for I am very well, but my weak faith still torments me."[52] He struggled to believe what he so openly—in the face of tremendous danger—taught and preached. Luther referred to these types of trials as his *Anfechtung*.

There is no direct English equivalent of the German word. In 1950, Roland H. Bainton described *Anfechtung* as "doubt, turmoil, pang, tremor, panic, despair, desolation, and desperation."[53] David Scaer acknowledged the many ways the word is translated, then stated, "*Anfechtung* is perhaps better understood not as one vocable in Luther's vocabulary, but as a one-word theological concept."[54]

Luther's Explanation of *Anfechtung*

Luther instructs about *Anfechtung* in his sermon on the Gospel story of the road to Emmaus (see Luke 24:13–35). Two disciples were talking about all that had happened the day Jesus rose from the dead. The risen Christ joined them. They did not recognize Him, even after He explained that what had happened was the fulfillment of the Scriptures, until He broke bread with them.

> From this we learn, first, that weakness and defects remain even in those who are now Christians. . . . Faith is not such a trifling or easy matter as foolish and inexperienced spirits imagine. . . . Christians and believers experience—both in others and in themselves—confess, and lament their weakness. . . . Thy have to fight and contend against their weakness all their lives.[55]

Luther thus says that *Anfechtung* is inevitable because it is so difficult to reconcile the difference between the reality of salvation and the reality of our sinful condition. But Luther says, "take heart," for Christ understands and has great compassion:

> But look at how He intentionally accepts these two who are weak in faith, cares for them, and does everything to aid their weakness and to strengthen their faith. Because He sees and knows that they had gone away from the other apostles troubled and sad, not knowing what they should think or hope, He does not want to leave them stuck, remaining in such doubt and temptation.[56]

AN IMPORTANT DISTINCTION: *ANFECHTUNG* IS NOT MENTAL ILLNESS

Luther distinguished *Anfechtung* and mental health problems. Luther taught that *Anfechtung* was essential to faith, even though it is emotionally distressing. It has the salubrious effect of driving us to Christ's cross to pray that the Holy Spirit strengthen our faith. We are the weeping disciple who fell to his knees and begged Jesus, "I believe; help my unbelief" (Mark 9:24). Luther wrote, "I would like to write a book about *Anfechtung*. Without it no man can rightly understand the Holy Scriptures or know what the fear and love of God is all about. In fact, without *Anfechtung* one does not really know what the spiritual life is."[57] He is likewise recorded at the table by John Schlaginhaufen on December 11, 1531: "God both loves and hates our afflictions. He loves them when they provoke us to prayer. He hates them when we are driven to despair by them."[58] *Anfechtung* is inevitable, but it is not mental illness.

In the same way, mental illness is not an indication of spiritual problems. Mental health problems can happen to those confident in their faith. Consider the many persons in the Bible who talked directly with God but nonetheless had fear and sadness, including Abraham, Moses, Elijah, Jonah, Peter, and so many others. Persons in emotional distress may doubt that God loves them and may avoid doing things good for their spiritual life, such as going to church. Many with mental illness, however, are confident in their faith. This is perhaps best exemplified in the book *And She Was a Christian: Why Do Believers Commit Suicide?*[59] by Peter Preus, in which he writes about his wife's death by suicide due to serious mental health problems.

The Dangers of Relying on Emotion

Mental health problems and *Anfechtung* are distinct, but both are associated with emotional distress. Whether afflicted by mental health problems or by *Anfechtung*, Christians might get caught up in their subjective experience of distress and mistakenly question whether their faith is "good enough."

Many mistakenly believe that the idea of salvation and God's love should always cause them joy. They condemn themselves for their sin and because they do not feel the joy of salvation. This is, of course, contrary to what we believe about objective justification and about the source of our faith. Thus Luther says emotions are "obstacles to faith," since our sinful nature brings terror, which is difficult to reconcile with the joy of God's forgiveness. In his sermon on Luke 24, Luther says, "Before, their faith was hindered by fear and frightened thoughts; now what hinders it is their joy, which is much greater than was their previous fright."[60] Robert D. Preus writes of the fallacy of believing that feeling good is relevant to our salvation: "The troubled sinner . . . will not look inwardly to feelings, experiences or quality of faith to gain assurance that he or she is right with God. . . . Of course, justified sinners feel joy and at peace with God, but these emotions are the results, not the criteria, of their justification."[61]

Turning away from objective reality to the subjectivity of emotions is not new. Paul wrote, "I am astonished that you are so quickly deserting Him who called you in the grace of Christ and are turning to a different gospel— not that there is another one, but there are some who trouble you and want to distort the gospel of Christ" (Galatians 1:6–7). St. Augustine likewise condemned the idea that God's work needed to be felt in the human heart. He spoke of *incurvatus in se* (turned inward on oneself) to describe the preference being exhibited by some Christians to look inward for evidence of God's approval, rather than focusing outward on the saving work of God through the sacrificial death of Jesus Christ.

The Depredations of the Theology of Glory

In the Heidelberg Disputation of 1518, Luther said the "theologian of glory" prefers "works to suffering, glory to the cross, strength to weakness, wisdom to folly, and, in general, good to evil."[62] Contrary to Jesus' declaration, "It is finished" (John 19:30), these theologians of glory view Christ's suffering and death as incomplete. To these false teachers, Jesus' suffering was not enough to earn free forgiveness for sinners. Instead, to them, Jesus' suffering enables sinners to earn God's approval, to become, "Christlike" and follow "the example of Christ." They teach that we can have assurance that we are saved when our lives reflect the strength of our faith. More evil yet, they teach that suffering is a choice since it can be eliminated by strengthening our faith. According to these false teachers, *Anfechtung* has no place in the life of a believer, nor does emotional suffering. Anyone who experiences either must say to themselves, "The reason for my suffering is my lack of faith," and their suffering is magnified by guilt.

No one should casually dismiss the effects of the theology of glory. It is so pervasive that it goes unnoticed by many of us, but some hear it loud and clear. The person with depression, the mother of a daughter with schizophrenia, the traumatized child, and anyone else who experiences emotional distress must think, *I am not a good Christian*. In the face of such terrible teaching and consequent fear, victims of this perverse theology might be compelled to stop believing.

ANFECHTUNG AND MENTAL ILLNESS INFLUENCE EACH OTHER

Anfechtungen is distinct from mental health problems. The two, however, influence each other. *Anfechtung* is spiritual distress. By definition, distress is an emotion, and emotion is a psychological phenomenon. If *Anfechtung* is severe enough, the emotional distress will also be severe, and this can contribute to mental health problems.

Luther knew this and explicitly warned people against such thinking. At his table on December 11, 1531, he said, "God both loves and hates our afflictions. He loves them when they provoke us to prayer. He hates them when we are driven to despair by them."[63] Luther had personal experience of great physical torment causing depression. As previously noted, he wrote Melanchthon, "I had almost lost Christ and was thrown to the billows and buffeted by storms of despair so that I was tempted to blaspheme against God." This allowed him to write in sympathy to Jerome

Weller, "You say that the temptation is heavier than you can bear, and that you fear that it will so break and beat you down as to drive you to despair and blasphemy."[64] Likewise, to Prince Joachim of Anhalt, who had serious depression and anxiety, Luther wrote him not to think his illness was a reflection of poor faith: "I trust that Your Grace will have no doubts or perplexities about the creed or the gospel inasmuch as Your Grace has now been well instructed. . . . We must be weak, and are willing to be, in order that Christ's strength may dwell in us."[65]

In the opposite direction, anyone who suffers long with depression, anxiety, or an SPMI might question whether God loves them. Long-standing and serious emotional distress, like distress due to schizophrenia or serious depression, might tempt the person to question whether God is paying attention and knows their pain. So too, then, did Luther counsel people against developing spiritual doubt because of mental health problems. On February 19, 1532, Luther wrote to the burgomaster in Freiberg, Saxony, Valentine Hausmann:

> Accept this scourge as laid upon you by God for your own good, even as Saint Paul had to bear a thorn in the flesh, and thank God that He deems you worthy of such unbelief and terror, for they will drive you all the more to pray and seek help and say, as it is written in the Gospel, "Lord, help thou mine unbelief."[66]

In a subsequent letter to the same young man, dated June 24, 1532, Luther wrote, "Under no circumstances allow yourself to become impatient because you do not at once have strong faith." He cajoled, "God is not the kind of father who casts off sick and erring children; if He were, He would have no children."[67]

LUTHER'S INSIGHT INTO MENTAL HEALTH PROBLEMS FROM HIS *ANFECHTUNG*

Both *Anfechtung* and mental health problems can entail a disconnect from the truth. Doubt is the genesis of *Anfechtung*, as it leads to turmoil, despair, and panicked desperation. The next part of this book explains the association between mental health problems and thinking errors. The person with depression thinks himself unworthy of love, regardless of reality.

I strongly suspect that Luther's insight into the Gospel message gave him great awareness of thinking errors that contribute to mental health problems. When he thought wrongly about the meaning of the Gospel, he "hated the righteous God who punishes sinners." When he "began to understand that the righteousness of God is that by which the righteous lives by a gift of God, namely by faith," his emotional relief was profound. "I felt that I was altogether born again and had entered paradise itself through open gates." He then extolled the Gospel "with a love as great as the hatred with which I had before hated."[68]

It seems that in the same way, Luther recognized that errors in thinking can lead to depression and anxiety. As we will see in the following chapters, Luther counseled others to be cautious about trusting their own thinking. He knew that depressed persons, in particular, are often wrong in how they think.

PASTORAL CARE OF *ANFECHTUNG* AND MENTAL HEALTH PROBLEMS

Persons might experience *Anfechtung*, mental health problems, or both. Both *Anfechtung* and mental health problems will lead to emotional distress. However, they require different approaches to pastoral care.

Objective Justification, Private Confession, and Emotions

Pastoral care for *Anfechtung* cannot appeal to emotions. Certainly, we are reassured and experience joy that we are forgiven our sins in Christ. Whether we are happy or not, though, is irrelevant. Relying on subjective emotions—as the theologians of glory do—endangers our salvation by leading us away from the reality of objective justification.

When meeting with someone in distress, distinguish emotions and thinking. Ask them if they believe that their sins are forgiven. Pastors should strongly consider beginning such a meeting with private confession and absolution. Either the question brought forward by the person in distress or private confession and absolution could generate the opportunity to reassure the person of the objective reality of the forgiveness of sins.

When talking with someone in distress, remember to distinguish the objective and the subjective. Our justification is objective. Pastors should instruct parishioners (and parishioners should remind one another) that they should reject the subjectivity of emotional reasoning. Emotions cannot be trusted to reveal the truth. Remind them that regardless of how they feel, they are saved.

In contrast to the objective truth of the Bible, when talking with someone experiencing emotional distress associated with mental health problems, it can be difficult to convince persons that how they are thinking about themselves and others is incorrect. There are special strategies needed for such consolation, and they are covered in chapter 7.

Even to those in emotional distress, however, always offer spiritual consolation. In every letter he wrote, Luther began by reminding people of the catechism. God, using you as His messenger, can do what we mental health professionals cannot. You can remind those in emotional distress that God loves them and forgives their sins. Assure them that God is with them in their suffering. Remind them of the third article of the Apostles' Creed, which states that faith is a gift from God, not something that they themselves can control. If you are a pastor, remember that the power of the pastoral office far exceeds the power of mental health professionals.

Teach the Normalcy of Both *Anfechtung* and Mental Health Problems

Always attack the theology of glory by reminding those suffering that their suffering is not due to weakness of faith. Remind them that believing does not necessarily bring them the emotion of happiness. Once, while at the table, Luther was asked how to counsel those who do not experience that peace that the godly have according to the text: "Therefore, since we have been justified by faith, we have peace with God through our Lord Jesus Christ" (Romans 5:1). Luther replied, "Such a person should first be admonished so that he might understand that the Christian life is to be lived amid sorrows, trials, afflictions, deaths, etc." When pressed about the notion of peace, Luther reminded those at the table that peace is an objective reality, not an emotional experience: "It is true, they have peace in faith, but it is invisible and beyond our senses . . . according to the flesh and the senses they suffer the greatest disquietude and disturbance. So David complains, 'There is no rest in my bones,' and Christ did not experience peace on the cross."[69]

You can remind them also of the suffering of Moses, Job, David, Peter, Paul, and others. Remind them that suffering is essentially promised to the believer. The Lord promises Abraham that he would be the father of many nations, and then said, "Then the LORD says to Abram, 'Know for certain that your offspring will be sojourners in a land that is not theirs and will be servants there, and they will be afflicted for four hundred years'" (Genesis 15:13). Likewise, Christ says to His followers, "In the world you will have tribulation" (John 16:33) and, "If anyone would come after Me, let him deny himself and take up his cross and follow Me" (Matthew 16:24). Also remember that Christ says to His followers, "But take heart; I have overcome the world" (John 16:33). Regardless of the distress that you or those around you experience, Christ, on the cross and through the empty tomb, has overcome the power of sin, death, and hell for you.

LUTHER'S LAST LETTERS TO KATIE

Luther was not afraid of negative emotions. The records show how he never scolded anyone for grief and was open about his own. He wrote Melanchthon on June 5, 1530, of the death of his father a week earlier, "This death has cast me into deep mourning . . . [His passing has] caused so deep a wound in my heart that I have scarcely ever held death in such low esteem."[70]

We know of two letters that Luther wrote to his wife from Mansfeld, where he had traveled to mediate a dispute. His health was bad, as was the winter weather. She was worried about his health. His responses[71] are an excellent example of how Luther reassured the anxious with both the reality of Scripture and personal kindness.

In a letter dated February 7, 1546, he wrote her, "Do not plague me any longer with your worries. I have a better worrier than you and all the angels. He lies in a cradle and clings to a virgin's breast." He also addressed her worries about him, saying, "We are living well here." He wrote that he was provided with much good wine, joking, "I sometimes share it with my companions."[72] He knew a display of humor would assure her.

In another letter, written a week before he died, he addressed "the pious and anxious lady, Mrs. Catherine Luther." He told her that her worry had apparently not done much good, teasing, "While you have been worrying about us, we were almost consumed by a fire . . . (and yesterday) a stone almost fell on our heads."[73] He ended with a joke about the paradoxical consequences of her worrying: "I fear that if you do not stop worrying, the earth will swallow us up and all the elements will fall upon us." Then he concluded with a serious note about faith: "Is this the way in which you have learned the catechism and understand faith?"[74]

Luther took the same attitude—with Katie and with all—that Christ took about worries. On the one hand, Jesus admonished the disciples to not worry about things that may distress us in life (see Matthew 6:25–34). On the other hand, when Jesus' friend Lazarus died, and his sisters and loved ones were in great distress, Jesus wept with them (see John 11:5). Following Jesus' example, Luther admonished people against worry and always used worry as an opportunity to preach the Gospel. But he did not ever scold worry as anything less than part of the fallen human experience.

Chapter 6

Thoughts, Behaviors, and Mental Health Problems

Do not be conformed to this world, but be transformed by the renewal of your mind, that by testing you may discern what is the will of God, what is good and acceptable and perfect. Romans 12:2

Chapter 2 covered the distinctions between and the mutual influences of thoughts, behaviors, emotions, roles, and relationships. This chapter examines how thoughts and behaviors are learned, as well as how they can become habitual. It presents the way that thoughts and behaviors both determine and are determined by mental health problems. Chapters 7 and 8 then present Luther's advice within these contexts.

THOUGHTS, BEHAVIORS, EMOTIONS, ROLES, AND RELATIONSHIPS REDUX

Thoughts, behaviors, and emotions are closely related and influence how we do in our roles and within our relationships. Mental illness is defined as a mix of thoughts, behaviors, and feelings that cause distress, problems in roles and relationships, or both.

This section shows how we think and behave are learned and can become so habitual that they essentially sink out of awareness. Habits of thinking can be inaccurate, and behavior habits can be unhealthy. Since thoughts and behaviors are learned, however, they can be relearned to promote mental health.

The importance of thinking and behavior, in particular, was not discovered or unearthed by Luther, much less by twentieth-century mental health professionals. Millennia of scholars, biblical authors, including David and Paul, and many others have recognized their importance. As we will see, though, Luther is unique in applying these principles so insightfully to help those in emotional distress.

Thoughts and Behaviors Are Learned

Thoughts and behaviors are learned. Children learn quickly and intensively. Thus, important ways of thinking and behaving are largely learned in childhood.

We intentionally teach children some thoughts and behaviors. We teach children the Bible and how to think about it. We hope they learn what the catechism teaches. We help them understand the importance of being kind. We intentionally teach many behaviors or skills, including how to read, do math, pray, go to church, shoot a free throw, ride a bike, swim, drive a car, and so forth. Other behaviors they hopefully learn and practice include being gracious, polite, grateful, and other social skills needed to form and maintain relationships, knowing how to defend one's faith, eating healthy, exercising regularly, and controlling anger and other negative emotions.

Many important things that children learn are neither taught nor learned intentionally, however. They are learned by experience, including observation. For example, parents do not need to teach their children to talk. Effortlessly, between their first and sixth birthdays, children learn to talk and even more to hear. They develop a receptive vocabulary of about ten thousand words, learning about five new words a day over a five-year span.[75]

In the same way, children are born ready to learn about love. Children instinctively learn about themselves, others, and relationships. They learn from experience whether they are considered lovable and worth attention. They learn whether others can be trusted to take care of them. They learn to trust, or not to trust, that loving relationships are possible. Babies are born needing to be held, cuddled, and comforted. When supplied this by loving adults, they learn about love. It would be wonderful to think that all children learn that they are loved because they are lovable and that other persons can be trusted not to hurt them intentionally. The ACEs studies, however, tell us otherwise. The ACEs studies show us that what we learn in childhood has a tremendous impact throughout our lives (see chapter 1).

THOUGHTS AND BEHAVIORS BECOME HABITUAL: SLOW AND FAST THINKING

Some thoughts and behaviors become habitual to the extent that they happen automatically and essentially disappear from awareness. We know from research by cognitive psychologists that these habits are necessary for day-to-day functioning. Once we have learned a language, we do not have to think about what someone is saying to us. The words are automatically understood and processed. Reading about a new subject, such as theology, can be challenging the first time. With time and familiarity, reading gets more efficient and effective. We read faster and retain more.

Similarly for behaviors, they can become habitual to the point that we might barely pay attention to their execution. We do not have to remind ourselves how to climb stairs. We just climb them. We do not need to relearn how to make coffee and toast in the morning. We do not have to concentrate intensively, as we once did, when driving a car. At one point, all of these skills (listening, understanding, reading, climbing stairs, driving) had to be learned. This illuminates the difference between two thinking systems, as described by cognitive psychologist Daniel Kahneman in his book *Thinking, Fast and Slow*.[76]

Slow Thinking

The slow thinking system is deliberate. This type of thinking requires effort and attention. When learning a new skill, we must concentrate on what we are doing, engaging our slow thinking system. When faced with the cognitive challenge of an important task, we engage our slow, deliberate thinking system. If engaged in a heated or important conversation, we listen carefully, pay attention to what is said, and consider our response. When judging applicants for a job, we deliberately slow our thinking to consider the match between qualifications and the job duties. If driving in a new city, we turn off the radio to concentrate on the match between directions and the environment.

Fast Thinking

Much of our cognitive activity entails much faster, practically automatic thinking. When engaging in fast thinking, we think and engage in certain behaviors with minimal attention or effort.

Fast thinking capacity develops with experience, such as understanding words spoken or written in a language we know well. Fast thinking also happens with regard to how we understand other people. We can detect that someone is angry or sad by the slightest hint in their voice. The fast system is almost completely involuntary. It is impossible to not understand words spoken in a language we know. It is impossible not to read words we recognize on a page. It is impossible to not hear hurt or disappointment in a loved one's voice.

Fast thinking applies to behavior as well. Over time, with repetition and learning, many skills move from the slow, deliberate system to the fast system. In this way, sophisticated behaviors can become habitual. After a certain amount of experience, we can make coffee, type, or drive a car with little or no cognitive effort.

Put another way, fast thinking is knowing. I know how to drive a car, how to type, how to read, how to talk, and how to think about myself. We don't think about whether our children should go to school; we know they should. My grandson does not yet know how to play the piano, but he is learning. If he sticks with it, he will eventually know how to play.

In a very real sense, then, fast thinking is not thinking at all but rather simply reacting based on what we have learned and now know.

To summarize, with practice or experience, intentional thoughts and behaviors in our slow thinking system move into our fast thinking system and become knowledge and habits. We do not think about certain things because we do not have to think about them. Many persons are thus not consciously or actively aware of how they think and behave. This is particularly problematic when their habitual thoughts and behaviors are causing or contributing to emotional problems.

THOUGHTS CAN BE INACCURATE, AND BEHAVIORS CAN BE UNHEALTHY

Slow, deliberate thinking can be wrong. Even if we put effort into our choices and decisions, we still can make mistakes. We purchase an expensive item that we later regret. We send a child to a college we thought was good but turned out otherwise. Or we choose a treatment option for our illness that proves ineffective. Overall, however, when we engage in slow thinking, we are much more likely to realize our own thinking problems and errors.

Inaccurate fast thinking is much more likely and thus much more common. We have all experienced mistaken first impressions of another person, like learning that someone we first thought unfriendly is actually very shy. Congratulating a woman on her pregnancy when she is actually not expecting is a mistake many of us have made, as we allowed fast thinking to guide our rather regrettable words. Inaccurate fast thinking leading to prejudiced ideas about a group, such as certain racial and ethnic minorities, is commonly "known" by some.

In similar fashion, habits of behavior can be quite unhealthy. Hence we have the term *bad habits*. These might include smoking, a sedentary lifestyle, and unhealthy dietary habits. It might also include isolating oneself when depressed or excessively drinking in the face of stress.

Importantly, if someone's fast thinking is inaccurate, he or she is unlikely to realize it unless it is pointed out. In the same way, bad habits can become so ingrained that their negative effect on health is no longer appreciated.

TWO EXAMPLES

To summarize, there is a deterministic association between thoughts, behaviors, and emotions. The way we think, in particular, strongly influences how we feel and what we do. The way we think and behave is learned, and much of the learning occurs in childhood. Much thinking and behavior becomes "fast" or habitual because they have been learned so well. Habits of thinking and behavior thus tend to occur outside of our awareness. Thoughts become something that we simply know, and behaviors become habits.

Whether fast (automatic) or slow (deliberate), thinking can be inaccurate. Whether intentional or habitual, behaviors can be unhealthy. Fast thinking is not easily recognized as inaccurate, and behavioral habits are not always seen as unhealthy.

To anticipate chapters 7 and 8, someone experiencing an emotional problem must pull their thinking out of the fast system and consider it more carefully. He or she might likewise have to think about and change his or her habitual behaviors. Quincy and Melissa demonstrate these.

Quincy's Depression

Quincy had repeated negative experiences in childhood. His mother was an alcoholic. His father was regularly verbally abusive and occasionally physically abusive, especially when Quincy became a teenager. Quincy was born ready to be loved, but he did not experience it. He learned that he was unlovable and that those who are supposed to be loving can be cruel. Now an adult, Quincy spends much time thinking that he is unworthy and unlovable, leading to feelings of depression and isolating behaviors. He has never dated. Although often invited, Quincy rarely goes out with colleagues after work. If Quincy confided this in you, what might you do?

Melissa's Anxiety

Because she is shy, Melissa did not have many friends in school. In sixth and seventh grade, she was bullied by some girls at her school. As a result, she developed the habit of thinking others don't like her and don't want to be in her company. These thoughts cause her to feel chronically anxious in front of others. She moved two years ago and is now a member of your church. After much encouragement from the pastor at her previous church, she sang in the choir and went to Bible study every Sunday. Her thinking is still causing anxiety, though, and she has not joined the choir in her new church. She comes to Bible study, but her shyness and anxious thinking interfere with her making friends. Actually, many people like her, but she does not realize this. Might you be able to say something kind to Melissa to help her?

QUINCY'S AND MELISSA'S THOUGHTS, BEHAVIORS, EMOTIONS, ROLES, AND RELATIONSHIPS

Both Quincy and Melissa have deep-rooted thoughts about themselves. They "know" certain things about themselves. The wrong knowledge or beliefs about themselves greatly influence their emotional functioning and their behavior. Their knowledge about themselves, however, is wrong.

In fact, many people are quite fond of Quincy. He is well-liked because he is polite, thoughtful, kind, hardworking, and considerate. This reality is contrary to Quincy's fast-thinking system, and he does not perceive this. The reality is that Melissa did have friends in school, although not as many as some other girls, but she was too shy to think clearly and deliberately. A related reality is that she is very likable and has many people at church who, although they do not know her as well as they would hope, do like her.

Luther did not know either Quincy or Melissa. They are products of my imagination, based on hundreds of patients I have counseled over the years. He did know versions of them, though. Luther would have advised them in the same way that I advised various versions of Quincy and Melissa over the years. Luther would have advised: become aware of thinking, strive to realize when thinking is wrong, think more correctly, and engage in healthy behaviors.

How exactly Luther did that—and how you might likewise do that—will be covered in the next two chapters.

Chapter 7
Luther's Cognitive Advice

If there is any excellence, if there is anything worthy of praise, think about these things. Philippians 4:8

This chapter reviews thinking and mental health problems. After considering some biblical points about proper and improper thinking, it discusses how Luther advised people about their thinking. This chapter concludes by placing his advice into the context of the modern day. It also offers ideas for readers to do the same.

THINKING IN THE BIBLE

Thoughts are a big topic in the Bible. What people think has big implications in matters of life and death, both temporal and eternal. The Bible's message is threefold: be aware of your thinking, beware of false thinking, and think correctly.

Be Aware of Your Thinking

The Bible admonishes spiritual laziness associated with being unaware of thinking. Christ warns that we should be awake and aware. In a parable, He calls virgins who were thoughtful and prepared wise, whereas the unprepared He calls foolish. Both groups became drowsy and slept, but the wise virgins had thought ahead and prepared. "Watch therefore, for you know neither the day nor the hour" (Matthew 25:13). In like manner, Christ says, "Be ready, for the Son of Man is coming at an hour you do not expect" (Luke 12:40). Paul encourages us to "be watchful, stand firm in the faith" (1 Corinthians 16:13) and, "So then let us not sleep, as others do, but let us keep awake and be sober" (1 Thessalonians 5:6).

Beware of False Thinking

We must beware of foolish thinking and the false words of others. Instead, "Trust in the LORD with all your heart, and do not lean on your own understanding" (Proverbs 3:5). Paul admonishes, "We destroy arguments and every lofty opinion raised against the knowledge of God, and take every thought captive to obey Christ" (2 Corinthians 10:5).

Since humanity's fall into sin, our thinking is not godly. God says, "For My thoughts are not your thoughts, neither are your ways My ways, declares the LORD" (Isaiah 55:8) and, "From within, out of the heart of man, come evil thoughts, sexual immorality, theft, murder, adultery, coveting, wickedness, deceit, sensuality, envy, slander, pride, foolishness" (Mark 7:20–22).

Think Correctly

We must strive to think correctly. Paul's epistle to the Romans reproaches false thinking and encourages proper thinking: "Do not be conformed to this world, but be transformed by the renewal of your mind. . . . I say to everyone among you not to think of himself more highly than he ought to think, but to think with sober judgment, each according to the measure of faith that God has assigned" (Romans 12:2–3).

Paul likewise encourages proper thinking: "I appeal to you, brothers, by the name of our Lord Jesus Christ, that all of you agree, and that there be no divisions among you, but that you be united in the same mind and the same judgment" (1 Corinthians 1:10); and, "Finally, brothers, whatever is true, whatever is honorable, whatever is just, whatever is pure, whatever is lovely, whatever is commendable, if there is any excellence, if there is anything worthy of praise, think about these things" (Philippians 4:8).

Of course, Proverbs is a long recitation of proper thinking, telling the difference between wisdom and folly, between good and evil. It is written, "For the LORD gives wisdom; from His mouth come knowledge and understanding" (Proverbs 2:6); "The fear of the LORD is the beginning of wisdom" (Proverbs 9:10); and, "A fool takes no pleasure in understanding, but only in expressing his opinion" (Proverbs 18:2).

COGNITIONS AND MENTAL HEALTH PROBLEMS

Cognitions include how we think presently, how we remember the past, how we perceive the present, and how we anticipate the future. Thoughts determine our behaviors and emotions, as well as how we do in roles and relationships. If we think badly about ourselves, we will feel badly about ourselves. If we think badly about relationships and believe others will hurt us, we will feel anxious about forming relationships. Such anxiety will lead us to avoid relationships, which will make our depression even worse. If we think pessimistically about the future—expecting that things will not work out for us, that good things will turn bad—this, too, can cause depression and anxiety.

In terms of fast and slow thinking, if someone thinks these ways often and long enough, he or she will soon "know" them to be true. The knowledge will make the person perpetually anxious and chronically depressed. It will also affect how he or she behaves.

This is not new. Marcus Aurelius (121–180 AD) wrote that we are not bothered by things but by our "estimate" of them.[77] In other words, bad events don't cause people to become distressed, but their interpretation of what happened might. Losing a job is a temporary setback to Donna, but it is a crippling blow and a betrayal to Dave. The same event is thought about differently, and the different thoughts lead to different reactions. If you were friends with Dave, would you encourage him to reconsider his thinking? If so, you could have invented cognitive therapy.

COGNITIVE THERAPY
FOR MENTAL HEALTH PROBLEMS

Therapy about thinking is called cognitive therapy. Let's reiterate the principles of cognitive therapy. First, thinking can become habitual so that we become unaware of what we think. Second, thinking affects how we feel and what we do. Third, thinking can be wrong. Fourth, thinking is learned and, thus, can be relearned.

These principles lead to the strategies used by mental health professionals. The following strategies overlap. They are presented in no particular order.

Psychoeducation

Like all other versions of education, psychoeducation is telling people things they do not know. Psychoeducation is educating people about their psychological functioning. This is particularly important for persons in emotional distress. These persons need to be educated about the association between thinking, emotions, and behavior. Relatedly, they need to be encouraged to realize that they are likely unaware of their thinking and that their thoughts are sometimes erroneous.

Gentle Confrontation

Confrontation entails challenging the validity of thinking. This must be done gently because people do not enjoy learning that their thoughts are wrong. Confrontation involves showing them examples of how thinking can easily be wrong and gently pointing out examples of their incorrect thinking. An important strategy is to strongly encourage someone to share their thoughts with trusted friends or loved ones, then ask them how they would evaluate their accuracy. This may quickly demonstrate erroneous thinking. For example, a friend might gently say to someone, "You think you are not loved? How foolish. I love you. Many people love you."

Acceptance

Acceptance is the opposite of resistance. It means accepting that one is prone to incorrect thinking. Once a person realizes this, he or she can contest and struggle against the thoughts. Acceptance can happen only after the person is confronted by the errors of his or her thinking. It might be difficult, and it will likely take time. Negative thoughts cause depression, anxiety, and other mental health problems, but human nature is arrogant. It is hard to accept that what we "know" is wrong, even when that knowledge (such as, "I am unlovable") causes emotional distress. Thus acceptance is easier for someone when confrontation is done with gentleness. Acceptance can be encouraged by pointing out that erroneous thinking is inevitable. Mental health professionals utilize the strategies Luther utilized: normalization and depersonalization.

Normalization

Mental health problems are experienced as odd and shameful, especially since they are not talked about openly. Those suffering from mental health problems believe themselves different. To normalize mental health problems, empathize with people in their distress. Talk about and name what they are experiencing, then express directly that there is nothing unusual about the experience of mental health problems.

Depersonalization

Depersonalization is making foreign something afflicting us. It entails pushing something outside of oneself, as if it were not part of us and had been foisted upon us. If something is not part of us, it is easier to recognize it as alien, challenge it, despise it (as Luther would say), and defeat it. This is obvious with some medical illnesses. We can easily conceptualize how a cancerous tumor is attacking us or how a virus is invading us. This is harder to do with mental health problems because our thoughts and emotions are uniquely our own. Mental health professionals encourage persons with depression and anxiety to realize, "This depression is not you!" Luther depersonalized by referring to depressing thoughts as the evil work of Satan assailing someone.

Restructuring, Reframing, and Ignoring

After a habitual thought is pulled into awareness, examined, and found to be erroneous, its power over feelings and behavior can and must be diminished. Restructuring and reframing are strategies for changing thinking. An alternative strategy is simply ignoring such negative thoughts.

Restructuring

A misleading thought is restructured when it is replaced by a more realistic thought. For example, the thought, "No one likes me" can be replaced with, "Not everyone likes me, but many do like me." The thought, "I am going to do poorly at this task" can be replaced with, "I will try to do well, although I cannot control everything." A restructured thought acknowledges reality ("not everyone likes me"), but it is more balanced and realistic.

Reframing

Reframing is more drastic. We "frame" events and incidents by how we think about why they happened. Kim's friend does not say hello, and she thinks it is because her friend no longer likes her. Ken's boss is rude, and he thinks she is rude to him only. Both events, however, can be reframed by thinking an entirely different thought: Kim's friend was not ignoring her. Rather, she was distracted and did not see her; Ken's boss is simply rude to everybody.

Ignoring

At times, thoughts cannot be changed. Some are persistent because they are habitual and well-learned. They come unbidden and keep coming even if we try to change them. It is easy to imagine that someone raised his entire childhood in a verbally abusive household might be unable to stop thinking, "I am bad" and, "I never do anything right." Fortunately, restructuring or reframing is not necessary to diminish the influence of thoughts. Someone who is aware of negative thoughts and recognizes them as erroneous can ignore them. He or she can tell himself or herself, "I may not be able to stop my negative thinking, but I do not have to believe my negative thinking."

LUTHER'S USE OF MODERN COGNITIVE THERAPY TECHNIQUES

Each of the following examples is taken from Luther's letters and his talks at the table. In each, he advised about mental health problems. He used all of the strategies just mentioned.

"Mrs. M, you have been forgiven, whether you think so or not."

Luther addressed a January 11, 1543, letter to "Mrs. M." As mentioned in the introduction, Tappert acknowledges that the exact recipient of this missive is unknown, but many believe it had been Margaret Eschat or Eschaus.[78] The letter's recipient was troubled by words she had spoken out of anger. Luther directly *confronted* her sin and her incorrect thinking. He used her language in the letter, bringing what she did out to the open. He needed her to read and confront her own words that, while sinful and unkind, were not unforgivable. He confronted her erroneous thinking.

> Your brother John informs me that the evil spirit is troubling you because these wicked words slipped from your lips: "I wish that all those who brought it about that my husband was made burgomaster would go to the devil!" Your brother tells me that the evil spirit is tormenting you and making you believe that on account of these words you must remain in the devil's power forever. . . . Certainly it was not Christ who put into your mind

the notion that you belong to the devil, for Christ died in order that those who belong to the devil may be released from his power . . . you must not believe your own thoughts, nor those of the devil.[79]

"Prince Joachim, enjoying life is not a sin."

Prince Joachim of Anhalt had a serious and persistent depression. His distress was compounded by his incorrect idea that enjoying life was sinful. Luther wrote on May 23, 1534, and warned the prince against thinking incorrectly.

It is my opinion that Your Grace is reluctant to be merry, as if this were sinful. . . . Be merry, then, both inwardly in Christ Himself and outwardly in His gifts and the good things of life. He will have it so. It is for this that He is with us. It is for this that He provides His gifts—that we may use them and be glad.[80]

Luther *directly confronted* the errors of the way the prince was thinking. A month later, he wrote again to point out the erroneous way that the prince was thinking, using examples from the Bible. Luther *normalized* enjoyment of life and of music in particular to confront the anxiety-provoking way Joachim thought about enjoying life. Luther strove to *normalize* the joy experienced by socializing with others and having fun. He wrote, on June 26, 1534, "The saints made themselves joyful with psalms and stringed instruments."[81]

In the same letter, Luther *educated*. He corrected incorrect thinking about recovery and *normalized* that recovery can be slow. All persons with depression and anxiety think that their recovery is taking too long, and it is certainly true that recovery from a painful illness always takes too long. But Luther argued against another thought common to depression and anxiety, which is that recovery will never happen. Luther used his own experiences to emphasize how he knew that slow recovery is normal. He wrote,

I have every expectation that Your Grace's condition will improve, although improvement may be slow. . . . Meanwhile I remember that when I was sick it some-times took a longer time and sometimes a shorter time before I was helped.[82]

Young Luther Counseled by Dr. Staupitz

Johannes von Staupitz (ca. 1468–1524) became vicar general of the reformed Augustinian Order, the monastery in Erfurt in 1503. Luther entered the monastery in 1505, and the two became close. Clearly they agreed on much, including the problem of indulgences and the notions of "grace alone" and "Christ alone," which Staupitz wrote about in his 1518 treatise *On the Love of God*. After ordination as a priest in 1507, Luther studied theology at the University of Erfurt. Obtaining his doctorate in 1512, Luther took a position as a theology professor at Wittenberg University, a position formerly held by Staupitz.

Luther's affection for the older man surely also reflected that Staupitz helped him psychologically. Staupitz advised Luther several times that thoughts are not necessarily to be believed. Staupitz *confronted* young Luther about trusting his own thinking about theological matters, his personal speculations, as opposed to what was recorded in the Bible. In a Table Talk recorded by Caspar Heydenreich on February 18, 1542, Luther stated,

This is the way in which Staupitz comforted me when the devil was similarly vexing me: "Why do you trouble yourself with these speculations of yours?" Accept the wounds of Christ and contemplate the blood which poured forth from His most holy body for our sins.[83]

Staupitz had the same advice for Luther's thinking, which the older man knew was causing depression. Staupitz *reframed* Luther's thoughts. He encouraged young Martin to think that they were not correct but also that they were not evil. Luther wrote Jerome Weller in July 1530:

When I first entered the monastery it came to pass that I was sad and downcast, nor could I lay aside my melancholy. On this account I made confession to and took counsel with Dr. Staupitz (a man I gladly remember) and opened to him what horrible and terrible thoughts I had.

"Don't you know, Martin, that this temptation is useful and necessary to you? God does not exercise you thus without reason. You will see that He intends to use you as His servant to accomplish great things."[84]

"Jerome, you must depersonalize, accept, and ignore."

Most know that Luther turned from his intention to study law because of a terrifying thunderstorm. Apparently he convinced Hieronymus (Jerome) Weller to do the same, presumably not using the same method. At Wittenberg, Weller gave up the study of law to study theology. Luther invited Weller to stay in his home, where Weller tutored Luther's children. Weller was shy and depressed. In July 1530, he wrote Weller at the Luther residence. In the letter, Luther *depersonalized* depression. He attributed negative, depression-causing thoughts as being due to the corruption of the devil. He said,

Try as hard as you can to despise those thoughts which are induced by the devil. In this sort of temptation and struggle, contempt is the best and easiest method of winning over the devil. Laugh your adversary to scorn and ask who it is with whom you are talking.[85]

Conrad Cordatus likewise reported that Luther advised *depersonalization* at the table to those experiencing anxiety and depression. In autumn 1531, Luther said,

Those who are tempted by doubt and despair I should console in this fashion. First, by warning them to beware of solitude and to converse constantly with others about the Psalms and

Scriptures. Then (although this is hard to do, it is a very present remedy) let them persuade themselves if they can that such thoughts are really not theirs but Satan's, and that they should strive with all their might to turn their minds to other things and leave such thoughts to him.[86]

Luther also advised *acceptance* of tormenting thoughts, if necessary, but simultaneously *ignoring* them for being despicable and foolish. He advised against entering a disputation with evil, erroneous, anxiety- and depression-inducing thinking. "This devil is conquered by mocking and despising him, not by resisting and arguing with him. . . . In this way you will drive out your diabolical thoughts and take courage."[87]

In a previous letter to Weller dated June 19, 1530, Luther advised about the difference between accepting that negative thoughts are inevitable and allowing them to influence us.

Therefore beware, my Jerome, of letting them [Luther refers to bad thoughts] lodge in thy heart. A wise man in reply to one sorely tempted said: You cannot prevent birds fleeing [sic] over your head, but you can hinder them building in your hair.[88]

"Matthias, test your thinking with others."

Luther wrote the brother of his close friend Jerome Weller. Tappert tells us that Matthias Weller (1507–63) was apparently a gifted musician, evinced by his employ as organist at the cathedral in Freiberg, Saxony. Luther counseled Matthias to beware of his thinking and to share it with others who could point out the errors in his thoughts. On October 7, 1534, Luther wrote Matthias,

Your dear brother has informed me that you are deeply distressed and afflicted with melancholy. He will undoubtedly tell you what I have said to him. Dear Matthias, do not dwell on your own thoughts, but listen to what other people have to say to you. For God has commanded men to comfort their brethren, and it is his will that the afflicted should receive such consolation as God's very own.[89]

As noted above, Conrad Cordatus recorded Luther in autumn 1531, advising those experiencing "doubt and despair" to check their thoughts with others. He said, "I should console . . . by warning them to beware of solitude and to converse constantly with others about the Psalms and Scriptures."[90]

"Jerome, Joachim, and Elsa, there is nothing unusual about you."

Society takes a negative, stigmatizing view of those with mental illness. We do not often talk about mental health problems, and most people experience a general lack of familiarity with them. When someone experiences or develops depression, anxiety, or another mental health problem, he or she might think, *I only am like this. I am different. I am wrong. None can understand me.*

Apparently this type of thinking was also true in Luther's day. Luther often reassured persons in emotional distress that they are not alone. Indeed, he assured them that he himself had suffered as they suffer. To Jerome Weller, Luther wrote, "When I first entered the monastery it came to pass that I was sad and downcast, nor could I lay aside my melancholy."[91] To Prince Joachim, he wrote, "I myself, who have spent a good part of my life in sorrow and gloom."[92]

Elizabeth (Elsa) von Canitz was one of the nuns who fled the convent in Nimbschen in 1523. Through her aunt, Luther had asked Canitz to teach at a girls' school in Wittenberg. In subsequent direct correspondence, he wondered if she might be refusing because of depression. In a letter dated August 22, 1527, Luther *normalized* her depression and *educated* her that, while it might endure a while, it would eventually pass. Luther wrote:

I have in mind using you as a teacher for young girls. . . . I now ask you not to decline my invitation. I hear too that the evil one is assailing you with melancholy, O my dear woman, do not let him terrify you, for whoever suffers from the devil here will not suffer from him yonder. It is a good sign. Christ also suffered all this, and so did many holy prophets and apostles, as the Psalter sufficiently shows. . . . Willingly endure this rod of your Father. He will relieve you of it in His own good time.[93]

A Letter Containing Many of These Strategies

Jonas Von Stockhausen was the captain of mounted knights who policed the town of Nordhausen. The stress and his own health problems led the captain to become so depressed he was contemplating suicide. Luther wrote a compelling letter. Tappert provides us the letter Luther wrote him on November 27, 1532.[94]

The letter used many of the strategies previously reviewed in this chapter. Luther used (1) psychoeducation about the effects of thinking on emotions and behavior, about how fighting depression is both necessary and difficult, and about the need to be persistent. Luther (2) advised Von Stockhausen to confront his own thinking. He counseled (3) acceptance, (4) depersonalization, (5) normalization, (6) restructuring, (7) checking his thinking with others, and (8) ignoring his thoughts. I have underlined and numbered (referring back to the list of strategies in this paragraph) each particular strategy Luther used in this letter.

Good friends have informed me that the evil one is tempting you (4) severely with weariness of life and longing for death. My dear friend, it is high time that you cease relying on and pursuing your own thoughts (2). Listen to other people (7) who are not subject to this temptation. Give the closest attention (2) to what we say, and let our words penetrate to your heart. Thus God will strengthen and comfort you by means of our words.

At the outset you know that you should and must be obedient to God and carefully avoid disobedience to His will. Since you must be certain (1) and must understand that God gives you life and does not now desire your death, your thoughts should yield to this divine will, be obedient to it, and not doubt that your thoughts, being in conflict with God's will, were forcibly inserted into your mind (4) by the devil. Consequently you must resist them sternly and either suffer them (3, 8) or eradicate them (6) with like force. Our Lord Christ also found (5) life to be unpleasant and burdensome, yet He was unwilling to die unless it was His Father's will. He fled from death, held onto life as long as He could, and said, "My time is not yet come." Elijah, Jonah, and other prophets likewise found (5) life unendurable, cried out in their agony for death, and even cursed the day on which they were born, yet they had to fight against the weariness of life and continue to live until their hour had come. Such words and examples you must truly obey and imitate (1, 2) as words and admonitions from the Holy Ghost, and you must cast out and reject the thoughts (6) that impel you to act (1) otherwise.

And if it is hard for you to do (1) this, imagine that you are held fast (4) and bound by chains and that you must work (1) and sweat yourself out of their strangle hold by powerful exertions. For the darts of the devil cannot be removed pleasantly and without effort when they are so deeply imbedded (1) in your flesh. They must be torn out by force. Accordingly you must be resolute, bid yourself defiance, and say to yourself wrathfully (2, 6): "Not so, good fellow. No matter how unwilling you are to live, you are going to live and like it! This is what God wants, and this is what I want too. Begone, you thoughts of the devil (2, 4, 6)! To hell with dying and death! You will get nowhere with me," etc. Grit your teeth in the face of your thoughts, and for God's sake be more obstinate, headstrong, and willful than the most stubborn peasant or shrew—indeed, be harder than an anvil or piece of iron. If you impose such demands on yourself and fight against yourself (4) in this way, God will assuredly help you. But if you do not resist and oppose, but rather give your thoughts free reign to torment you, the battle will soon be lost.

But the best counsel of all is this: Do not struggle against your thoughts (3) at all, but ignore them (8) and act as if you were not conscious of them. Think constantly of something else (8), and say: "Well, devil, do not trouble me. I have no time for your thoughts. I must eat, drink, ride, go, or do this or that." In like manner say: "I must now be cheerful. Come back tomorrow," etc. Undertake to do anything else that you are able—whether play or something else—just so that you free yourself from these thoughts, hold them in contempt, and dismiss them (8). If necessary, speak coarsely and disrespectfully (8), like this: "Dear devil, If you can't do better than that, kiss my toe, etc. I have no time for you now." On this read the examples of the crackle of lice, the hissing of geese (8), and the like in Gerson's *De cogitationibus blaspkemiae*. This is the best counsel. In addition, our prayers and those of all godly Christians should and will also help you. Herewith I commit you to the keeping of our dear Lord, the only Saviour and real Conqueror, Jesus Christ. May He keep His victory and triumph over the devil in your heart. May He cause all of us to rejoice in the help He gives you and the miracle He performs in you. We confidently hope and pray for this in accordance with His command and promise to us. Amen.

COMMON TYPES OF NEGATIVE THINKING

Before moving on to applying cognitive strategies, there is one more topic to address. Some find it helpful to characterize types of thinking errors, including the following.

All-or-nothing thinking involves perceiving events only at the extremes. Things are either black or white, right or wrong, perfect or terrible.

Perfectionism is thinking that any event or performance that is not conducted perfectly is terrible. This thinking leads to depression related to the thought *I failed* and anxiety about being evaluated negatively.

Attending only the negative is the habit of focusing on small problems or imperfections while ignoring overall success.

Catastrophizing entails greatly exaggerating—making a catastrophe of—the importance of some minor problem or mistake.

Disqualifying the positive is to discount success as luck, good fortune as unusual, and praise and kindness as exceptions.

Mind reading is assuming to know what another person is thinking by the look they give you, their tone of voice, or just because you think you already know what everybody always thinks of you.

APPLYING COGNITIVE STRATEGIES AS LUTHER DID

You can apply Luther's ideas with confidence, knowing that they are consistent with what mental health professionals do today. Luther based his advice on common sense and compassion. You likely have both of these traits as well.

Psychoeducation

Educate others about *the association between thoughts, behaviors, and feelings.* The importance of thinking, in particular, is always underappreciated. Most persons simply do not pay much attention to thinking, especially if it is "fast" and habitual. Encourage someone in emotional distress to think about their thinking by educating them about the distinction between thoughts and feelings. Provide examples, including ones from your own life. Some examples include the following:

- "Is it more correct to say, 'I feel I purchased a bad computer' or 'I think I've purchased a bad computer'?"

- "Should Amy say, 'I feel Becky does not like me' or 'I think Becky does not like me'?"

- "If I think I've purchased a bad car, how will I feel?"

- "If Katie thinks that Martin doesn't like her, how will she feel?"

Teach that *thinking often happens outside of awareness*. Thoughts become so habitual that we do not notice them. You can give advice such as the following:

- "We all get in the habit of thinking certain thoughts."

- "Sometimes thinking is so well-learned, people aren't even aware of their thoughts."

- "Oftentimes we are unaware of our thinking."

- "People who are depressed get in the habit of thinking that they are not liked or are not lovable."

Listen for "should," which is an important clue to negative thinking. The person might say, "I should have known better to do that," or, "I should not have made that mistake." People who often use the word *should* are exhibiting perfectionism. Using *should* often can indicate someone prone to depression or anxiety.

Gentle but Firm Confrontation

Strive to help the person *confront* the reality that the way they think can be incorrect. *Be gentle but firm.* They are not thinking correctly and need a kind but firm friend to tell them so. Be confident, especially with clearly erroneous thinking. Be confident that he or she is loved by God, is not a bad parent, and is not always wrong. Be confident that perfection is impossible and that, in reality, few people expect perfection from others. Remind them that the only perfect human was Jesus, who died and rose again to give the gifts of His perfect life to us. Also be confident that most people are forgiving and kind.

Sometimes erroneous thinking is practically amusing, including thoughts like these:

- Bill says, "I am a bad employee," despite the fact that he was just promoted.

- Sarah thinks, "I'm a bad mom," even though her children get good grades, have many friends, and are loved by teachers.

- After being criticized by a member, beloved Pastor Tom thinks, "I'm a bad pastor."

With these and similar examples, you might respond with gentle amusement, "So help me understand. You were just promoted because you are a bad employee?"

Be kind, gentle, and empathic. People believe their thinking. They need kindness and patience to understand that their thinking is wrong. Some things that you might say kindly and gently—but firmly—include:

- "I'm not sure I agree with what you are thinking."

- "I think a lot of people might doubt what you are saying about yourself."

- "You tend to think very badly of yourself."

- "It is important to know that you are thinking incorrectly about yourself."

Acceptance

Helping someone accept their thinking and its effect on their feelings and actions takes time. Be firm and persistent, but also be patient. Be aware that *they might think you are criticizing.* They might think that you are saying their distress is their fault. Assure them that you are not being critical. Use normalization to communicate that faulty thinking is commonplace.

Contradict the theology of glory by reminding them that the experience of pain does not mean they have weak faith. Remind the person that we are all flawed. Encourage them to accept that they do not have to be perfect. Remind them that Jesus died and rose again to forgive their imperfections, both large and small. Insist that it is essential to both their mental and spiritual health to be okay with being wrong in this vale of tears. Remind them what the Bible says, using questions such as these:

- "What did Christ mean when He said, 'Take up [your] cross daily and follow Me' (Luke 9:23)?"

- "Do you remember how Moses and David suffered? How about Paul? Peter?"

- "God does not expect us to be perfect. We are all flawed, 'for all have sinned and fall short of the glory of God' (Romans 3:23). Christ died to make us perfect before God. His grace is sufficient for us, for His power is made perfect in our weakness (2 Corinthians 12:9)."

Depersonalization

Depersonalization can be suggested only after the person accepts that their thinking is wrong. Distancing oneself from negative thinking makes it easier to combat it. Depersonalization is a particularly useful strategy when the person talks about being victim to their thinking, such as, "I cannot stop these thoughts." You can suggest the following:

- "Our thoughts can be hard to control, but we don't have to listen to our thoughts."

- "Sometimes we think things that are absurd. Do you ever do that? Do you ever get the sense that your thoughts are being directed by your depression?"

- "Luther compared his erroneous thinking to honking geese and the cracking of lice. What do you think he meant by that?"

Normalization

Normalization assures the person that distress due to a mental health problem is common. You can do this by giving examples of others with similar problems. The best strategies to use for normalization are *psychoeducation* and *storytelling*. Present statistics and facts about mental health problems. Luther could not do this, but you can. Assure them that they are not alone, neither in society nor in the church. Simply say or ask the following:

- "I am sorry you are experiencing this. Many people do."

- "How many people here at church do you think have gone through—or are now going through—something similar to what you are experiencing?"

- "What you are experiencing is very, very common."

Storytelling is invaluable in normalization. *Tell personal stories*, especially stories from your own life and your experiences with others. *Tell stories from the Bible.* Remind them of the many who walked and talked with God directly and experienced emotional anguish. *Tell stories about Luther.* Examples include the following:

- "I have seen this in my family, among my friends, and here at church."

- Ask them to imagine the fear of Abraham when he instructed his wife to give herself to another man, or the distress of Moses when he asked God to take his life.

Restructuring Thinking

Once the person recognizes he or she is thinking incorrectly, directly advise that he or she *change his or her thinking.* Some are able to do this fairly readily. Others must develop the habit.

To become more aware, suggest he or she track his or her thinking on an index card or notepad he or she can carry with him or her. Suggest that he or she note the association between his or her thinking and his or her feelings. He or she can then evaluate how accurate his or her thinking is ("On a scale of one to ten, with ten being completely accurate, how logical, realistic or accurate would you rate that thought?") Strategies for restructuring our thinking can be readily found on the internet.

Ignoring Thinking

Changing or stopping erroneous thinking can be difficult. Thinking about our thinking in a new way, however, is relatively easy. As with depersonalization, this strategy will be effective only if the person accepts that thinking influences emotions and that thinking can be incorrect.

Encourage the person to realize that he or she can ignore his or her thinking. He or she may not be able to stop thinking, *Everyone hates me,* or, *I am always doing something wrong.* The person, though, does not have to *believe* those thoughts. No one must allow a thought the power to make them feel bad. Some of Luther's advice was much ahead of its time, sounding similar to advice dispensed in the twenty-first century. You can offer Luther-inspired advice such as the following:

- "Do not struggle against your thoughts at all, but ignore them and act as if you were not conscious of them."

- "Think constantly of something else."
- "Say, 'Devil, I have no time for your thoughts.'"
- "Hold these thoughts in contempt. Dismiss them."

The following chapter parallels this chapter. It describes how Luther helped persons with mental health problems develop better behaviors in order to feel better and do better.

CHRIST AND ANXIOUS THINKING

I end this chapter by offering a new way to think about a chapter from the Gospel that causes consternation and even guilt in persons who experience depression and anxiety. Because of the theology of glory, some might think that Christ condemns anxiety.

> Therefore I tell you, do not be anxious about your life, what you will eat or what you will drink, nor about your body, what you will put on. Is not life more than food, and the body more than clothing? Look at the birds of the air: they neither sow nor reap nor gather into barns, and yet your heavenly Father feeds them. Are you not of more value than they? And which of you by being anxious can add a single hour to his span of life? And why are you anxious about clothing? Consider the lilies of the field, how they grow: they neither toil nor spin, yet I tell you, even Solomon in all his glory was not arrayed like one of these. But if God so clothes the grass of the field, which today is alive and tomorrow is thrown into the oven, will He not much more clothe you, O you of little faith? Therefore do not be anxious, saying, "What shall we eat?" or "What shall we drink?" or "What shall we wear?" For the Gentiles seek after all these things, and your heavenly Father knows that you need them all. But seek first the kingdom of God and His righteousness, and all these

things will be added to you. Therefore do not be anxious about tomorrow, for tomorrow will be anxious for itself. Sufficient for the day is its own trouble. (Matthew 6:25–34)

The theologian of glory says Christ condemns and punishes us for foolish, erroneous thinking. The theologian of glory will preach that Christ condemns weak faith, as demonstrated in mental distress, and that in order to be saved we need to strengthen that faith. Satan wants us to think this way also. The devil would have you and me think that Christ came to condemn anxiety and other mental health problems as sin. As persons believe the lies of theologians of glory, Satan's efforts to cause despair and to weaken the faith of God's people are bolstered.

Luther thought otherwise. He condemned turning the Gospel into Law: "The devil makes a law of the Gospel."[95] He condemned those who condemned persons for their emotional distress. Luther's theology of the cross has much more comfort to offer.

A theologian of the cross views anxiety, emotional distress, and suffering differently. A theologian of the cross sees that even when we are anxious, God, who is in heaven, is in charge of everything. He or she sees that Christ came to perfectly obey the law on our behalf. By doing so, He satisfied God's anger at us. Despite our flawed thinking, we know Christ assures us that there is nothing to cause us anxiety. As with every other word He spoke, Christ assures us He has fulfilled the Law on our behalf. Our faith is too weak to grasp this, so we are comforted by knowing that faith is a gift of the Holy Spirit through God's Word and Sacrament. A theologian of the cross says, as the disciple said to Christ, "I believe; help my unbelief!" (Mark 9:24). A theologian of the cross clings to the Gospel in the midst of our broken world and broken thinking, trusting in and receiving God's gifts of forgiveness, life, and salvation through whatever we experience in life.

Chapter 8

Luther's Behavioral Advice

For I do not understand my own actions.
For I do not do what I want,
but I do the very thing I hate. Romans 7:15

This chapter reviews how behavior affects mental health. It starts with a review of what the Bible says about behavior. It discusses some of the ways Luther advised people about their behavior to help them with emotional distress, shows how his advice is consistent with modern advice, and suggests how readers can do what Luther did.

BEHAVIOR IN THE BIBLE

The Bible is replete with advice about behavior, including the behavior of the righteous and the need to support others. It warns about the danger of isolation, encouraging instead community and fellowship. It also has many examples of the value of solitude.

Honorable Conduct

Peter reminded the faithful of how eager nonbelievers are to mock and deride followers of Christ. He commended honorable conduct, writing, "Keep your conduct among the Gentiles honorable, so that when they speak against you as evildoers, they may see your good deeds and glorify God on the day of visitation" (1 Peter 2:12). Paul wrote the same to his companion Titus: "Show yourself in all respects to be a model of good works, and in your teaching show integrity, dignity, and sound speech that cannot be condemned, so that an opponent may be put to shame, having nothing evil to say about us" (Titus 2:7–8). To the church in Philippi, he wrote, "Only let your manner of life be worthy of the gospel of Christ, so that whether I come and see you or am absent, I may hear of you that you are standing firm in one spirit, with one mind striving side by side for the faith of the gospel" (Philippians 1:27).

Isolation

The book of Genesis tells us that while Adam was surrounded by the perfection of the Garden of Eden, the Lord God proclaimed, "It is not good that the man should be alone; I will make him a helper fit for him" (Genesis 2:18). And so God made Eve for Adam.

In Scripture, we are warned of how isolation is dangerous. Too much time with ourselves leads to improper thinking and associated emotions. For, "Whoever isolates himself seeks his own desire; he breaks out against all sound judgment" (Proverbs 18:1). Luther repeated St. Peter when he spoke of the devil as a prowling lion: "Be sober-minded; be watchful. Your adversary the devil prowls around like a roaring lion, seeking someone to devour" (1 Peter 5:8). When lions hunt, they seek to isolate. They cull a weak or young animal away from the herd so that they can kill and eat it. Thus does the company of others offer significant protection, physically for the beast and spiritually for us. Just so, when Christ sent out the disciples to confront demons, He did not send them alone: "And He called the twelve and began to send them out two by two, and gave them authority over the unclean spirits" (Mark 6:7).

Fellowship

Fellowship and communion are the opposite of isolation. They help sustain us when we are in doubt and make us stronger in the faith. The comfort and counsel of fellow believers builds us up in the true faith to better withstand the turmoil of the world. Thus, the Bible includes many verses about seeking out the company of other believers.

Christians are to help one another bear afflictions, including mental health problems. "Bear one another's burdens, and so fulfill the law of Christ" (Galatians 6:2). We are to encourage one another's faith. Only in fellowship do we spread the Good News. "Let each of you look not only to his own interests, but also to the interests of others" (Philippians 2:4). Only in fellowship can we support the weak. "We who are strong have an obligation to bear with the failings of the weak, and not to please ourselves" (Romans 15:1). In fellowship, our love is stirred up and our actions are emboldened. "And let us consider how to stir up one another to love and good works, not neglecting to meet together, as is the habit of some, but encouraging one another, and all the more as you see the Day drawing near" (Hebrews 10:24–25).

Quiet Time

It is not a contradiction to say that being alone for prayer and meditation can help our communion with God. Solitude can be salutary, especially for those whose work is great and need rest. Christ went off by Himself, to desolate (isolated) places, to be alone and pray. In grief over the death of His cousin, John, Christ set out to be alone. Compassion took Him back to feed those following Him, but then, "after He had dismissed the crowds, He went up on the mountain by Himself to pray" (Matthew 14:23). Perhaps because He was tired after a previous day's labor casting out demons and healing the sick, Jesus sought out communion with His Father: "And rising very early in the morning, while it was still dark, He departed and went out to a desolate place, and there He prayed" (Mark 1:35). Luke the physician seems to connect Christ's endless labor with Christ's frequent need to be alone to pray: "But now even more the report about Him went abroad, and great crowds gathered to hear Him and to be healed of their infirmities. But He would withdraw to desolate places and pray" (Luke 5:15–16).

To summarize, the Bible tells us that being alone is bad, except when it is done for our good. Isolating ourselves is dangerous, and receiving the gifts of God's Word within the community of saints is central to life within the Body of Christ. Being alone at times for prayer and meditation, however, is also important to the life of faith. It can help us recover when we are wearied of our burdens.

BEHAVIOR AND MENTAL HEALTH PROBLEMS

Persons with depression and anxiety have negative thoughts and negative emotions. These greatly affect behavior, leading to behavior that often maintains depression and anxiety. Behaviors that are particularly bad for mental health are social isolation and lack of participation in enjoyable activities, which leads to an unhealthy lifestyle.

Social Withdrawal and Isolation

Persons with mental health problems almost inevitably withdraw from others. This is because they look to future events and cannot imagine that they will enjoy themselves. This includes things that they've enjoyed in the past. Kara enjoyed dancing and going out with friends while she was in college. After her divorce from her college sweetheart, she became depressed. That led her to think that she would not enjoy going out with friends, so she now ignores invitations to do so. Norm used to enjoy golfing with friends. His surgery caused significant pain for about a year, and he became depressed. He is now physically able to golf again, but he has not reached out to friends.

Persons with anxiety can get into similar vicious cycles. Due to thinking that they will be anxious in a situation, they avoid the situation. As a result, they do not learn that the situation is not as dangerous or as scary as they imagine. Lisa is seven years old and afraid of her best friend's dog, Samson. Lisa will experience anxiety at the thought of going to her friend's house. She often declines an invitation to play there. Samson is actually friendly and playful, but Lisa never experiences that. As a result, her thinking—dogs are dangerous—does not go away, and her feeling of fear is never remedied.

Luther knew such bad habits. Luther got into the habit of avoiding the company of others when he was taken to the Wartburg fortress. He isolated himself from the others, and his depression worsened.

Enjoyable Things

Another emotional symptom of depression is apathy, which translates "without emotion." Apathy might be due to negative thinking or anticipating that an activity will not be enjoyable. It is hard to be motivated to do something when you do not anticipate enjoying yourself. Returning to the above example, Norm used to like golfing, but his depression makes him unable to anticipate that he will enjoy it again. Luther once reminded the gifted organist Matthias Weller to play the organ when he was assailed with depression. Luther offered such seemingly unnecessary advice because he knew persons with depression often do not do what they previously enjoyed doing. He wrote, "When melancholy threatens to get the upper hand . . . play a song unto the Lord."[96] One could speculate that if Luther had known John Calvin, he would have told him that he must ignore his negative expectation and do what was good for him.

Lack of enjoyment might be due to *anhedonia*, which translates as "without pleasure." Someone with *anhedonia* will engage in behavior that previously gave them pleasure and find that they no longer enjoy it. Thus does Luther so often cajole those with depression and anxiety, "You must go do fun things, such as ride, play music, play games, and so forth." Note that Luther was not saying, and you should not say, "You will have fun!" Rather, Luther was saying, as you should say, "Do it because it will be good for you."

Neglecting Health-Promoting Behavior

Related to these thoughts and emotions, persons with depression and anxiety will not engage properly in healthy behaviors. They will not exercise enough, they will not take the time to prepare healthy meals, and they may unintentionally develop poor sleep habits. The section titled "Self-Care Behaviors" in chapter 9 discusses strategies for redressing potential problems in this important area of life as an important way to combat depression and anxiety. This is not advice Luther gave, but it is important advice nonetheless.

Modern Life, the Business of the Family, and Being Too Busy for Fun

Modern life can cause depression because it is so busy that individuals, couples, and families neglect to do things that they enjoy. The words *busy* and *business* are related. There is much "business" in having a family, such as packing lunches, getting kids to school, paying bills, making meals, cleaning the home, maintaining vehicles, and so much more. Likewise, work outside the home keeps many adults busy. Technology allows work to follow us home, on laptops and cellphones, throughout the night, and into weekends.

It's a simple and common phenomenon: a couple unintentionally fails to attend to the thing that brings them the greatest joy, which is their relationship. They might "fast think" that the behaviors that bring them joy—going out together, having a meal by themselves—will happen spontaneously, as they did when they were dating. But they usually won't, unfortunately, because they are too busy. Thus their relationship inadvertently takes lower priority than children and the business of home and work, and their relationship unintentionally suffers.

To summarize, it is sensible and helpful to consider the joys of life as necessary to prevent or defeat depression and anxiety. The following discusses Luther's advice in this regard.

BEHAVIOR THERAPY
FOR MENTAL HEALTH PROBLEMS

Cognitive therapy is the dominant form of therapy because, like the eight-hundred-pound gorilla, it is powerful. It is the most widely studied and most widely practiced form of therapy. Behavior therapy, however, is also powerful and has some advantages over cognitive therapy. Luther's advice regarding behavior tended to be both brief and succinct, and he thus seemed to know the advantages.

Advantages of Advising about Behavior

Behavioral issues leading to mental health problems are easier to identify than cognitive errors. Behaviors can become habitual, but there is no "fast thinking" version of behavior. By definition, behavior is observable. Also, behaviors to combat mental health problems are straightforward. Behavioral advice entails the instruction "Do this" or, more fully, "Do this and then do that."

It is easy to evaluate whether someone has followed behavioral advice. Advice about changing thinking can be difficult to follow for the person or to evaluate by the counselor. Thoughts are often so habitual that becoming aware of and challenging them takes practice. In contrast, if you give someone advice about their behavior—if you tell someone to go to church, to do something fun, or to call a friend—it is easy for you to later ask whether they followed the advice. They will indicate whether they did or did not. They might say, "I meant to but did no," or, "I forgot," but they won't say, "I'm not sure whether I did that or not."

Behavioral Activation

Modern mental health professionals routinely give two pieces of behavioral advice to persons with depression and anxiety: go out with others and do fun things. Such behavioral activation is one of the most powerful treatments in existence, and it is available to everyone for free.

Although behavioral advice is easier to give than advice about thinking, implementing behavioral activation can be a challenge. This is because thinking (*It won't be fun*) and associated emotions (*I'm too down to do that*) are still at play when working to activate behavioral change. The strategies that mental health professionals use to increase the likelihood that someone will engage in behavioral activation focus, ironically, on thinking. Some strategies are listed below.

Helping persons recognize that the way they are acting is unhealthy for their mental health is essential. This strategy is fairly easy because unhealthy behavior is so formidably obvious. Few people can deny that isolation is unhealthy, and few would argue against the benefits of pleasurable activities. I once asked a young man with depression, a sophomore in college, what he did for fun the previous week. He thought for a moment, then said with a straight face, "On Friday, I did my laundry." I looked at him quizzically, then I burst out laughing. Soon he, too, was laughing. He realized the absurdity of what he said. He readily acknowledged that so seriously depriving himself of fun was unhealthy.

Helping persons ignore thinking and emotions that encourage unhealthy behavior is another strategy. Persons with depression do not anticipate enjoying things. Those with anxiety look to future events with anxiety-provoking thinking. These expectations will lead to isolation and avoidance.

For this reason, mental health professionals tell depressed and anxious patients that they must do enjoyable things, regardless of whether they anticipate (think) that they will have fun and regardless of how they feel. Consistent with the contents of chapter 7, someone with depression and anxiety must not heed his or her flawed thoughts or feelings. The cognitive strategy of depersonalization is relevant to this. The person cannot let the illness dictate his or her behavior. As Luther told Captain Von Stockhausen,

"Imagine that you are held fast and bound by chains and that you must work . . . out of their strangle hold by powerful exertions."[97]

Helping persons plan enjoyable activities is an essential strategy. This is contrary to how many normally behave, which is to do enjoyable things spontaneously. Persons with depression and anxiety cannot rely on spontaneity, however. They have baseline distressing thoughts and emotions. They do not anticipate enjoying anything and feel like doing nothing. Thus, they must plan enjoyable activities, perhaps days or more beforehand, and must stick to their plan. Hence an important, related strategy is to plan such activities with friends. Friends can be instructed to hold them to the scheduled activity. Commitment to friends is often more important than their negative expectations and emotions. Friends are happy to help, as they will recognize the need for the person to do fun things.

LUTHER'S MODERN ADVICE ABOUT BEHAVIOR

Some of Luther's advice regarding behaviors is presented as documented in his letters and his talks at the table. Luther dispensed modern-day behavioral advice. He distinguished socializing and avoiding solitude, advising both, and he encouraged fun. Typically, he encouraged all three in the same letter or talk.

"Dear tutor, flee solitude, socialize, and have fun"

We read about how Luther gave advice on thinking to his friend and tutor to his children, Hieronymus (Jerome), in chapter 7. Luther also gave this shy and often depressed man behavioral advice. In July 1530, while on a trip, Luther wrote him at the Luther residence to advise socialization, the most effective form of behavioral activation for combating depression.

By all means flee solitude, for the devil watches and lies in wait for you most of all when you are alone. This devil is conquered by mocking and despising him, not by resisting and arguing with him. Therefore, Jerome, joke and play games with my wife and others. . . . Seek out the company of men, drink more, joke and jest, or engage in some other form of merriment. Sometimes it is necessary to drink a little more, play, jest, or even commit some sin in defiance and contempt of the devil in order not to give him an opportunity to make us scrupulous about trifles.[98]

"You too, young Prince Joachim"

He encouraged Prince Joachim of Anhalt in the same way. (We also met Prince Joachim of Anhalt in chapter 7.) Luther believed the prince's persistent depression was related to his behavior. Because of incorrect thinking, the prince had withdrawn from the pleasure of the company of others. In a letter dated May 23, 1534, Luther was very direct in his advice:

I should like to encourage Your Grace, who are a young man, always to be joyful, to engage in riding and hunting, and to seek the company of others who may be able to rejoice with Your Grace in a godly and honorable way. For solitude and melancholy are poisonous and fatal to all people, and especially to a young man. . . . This is frequently asserted by Moses, and in Eccl, ch 12, we read, "Rejoice, O young man, in thy youth; and let thy heart cheer thee." No one realizes how much it does a young person to avoid pleasure and cultivate solitude and sadness.

Your Grace has Master Nicholas Hausmann and many others near at hand. Be merry with them; for gladness and good cheer, when decent and proper, are the best medicine for a young person—indeed, for all people.[99]

Notice that Luther gave specific advice about where to find boon companions. Perhaps Luther thought Prince Joachim needed such specific advice. I think it reads as gentle scolding at the possible excuses the prince might offer for not socializing. We can also take it as an example of advice reviewed earlier. It is important to plan fun things to make sure they happen.

In the same letter, Luther alerted the prince about how his thinking might affect his behavior. He used normalization, reviewed in chapter 7, to contradict the negative thinking leading to the prince's pursuit of solitude. He wrote,

> I myself, who have spent a good part of my life in sorrow and gloom, now seek and find pleasure wherever I can. Praise God, we now have sufficient understanding [of the Word of God] to be able to rejoice with a good conscience and to use God's gifts with thanksgiving, for he created them for this purpose and is pleased when we use them.[100]

Luther Condemned Solitude

At the table, Luther vehemently warned against solitude. In a talk recorded by John Schlaginhaufen in 1532, he stated that papists and Anabaptists taught that "if you wish to know Christ, you must seek solitude." He condemned the advice as "manifestly diabolical" and contrary to the Ten Commandments, as the first table "demands faith and fear of God" and the second demands "that his name be proclaimed and praised before men and spoken of among men." He called solitude "destructive of the family, economic life, and the state." He pointed out that Christ "was never alone except when He prayed."[101]

In the same Table Talk, Luther pointed out that behaviors affect the way we think and thus, the way we feel. At the table in 1534, he was recorded saying:

More and graver sins are committed in solitude than in the society of one's fellow men. The devil deceived Eve in paradise when she was alone. Murder, robbery, theft, fornication, and adultery are committed in solitude, for solitude provides the devil with occasion and opportunity. On the other hand, a person who is with others and in the society of his fellow men is either ashamed to commit a crime or does not have the occasion and opportunity to do so. . . . Christ was alone when the devil tempted Him. David was alone and idle when he slipped into adultery and murder. I too have discovered that I am never so likely to fall into sins as when I am by myself.

God created man for society and not for solitude. This may be supported by the argument that he created two sexes, male and female as, he continued, God likewise instituted the Sacraments, preaching, and consolations in the Church.

Solitude produces melancholy. When we are alone the worst and saddest things come to mind. We reflect in detail upon all sorts of evils. And if we have encountered adversity in our lives, we dwell upon it as much as possible, magnify it, think that no one is so unhappy as we are, and imagine the worst possible consequences. In short, when we are alone, we think of one thing and another, we leap to conclusions, and we interpret everything in the worst light. On the other hand, we imagine that other people are very happy, and it distresses us that things go well with them and evil with us.[102]

"Spite your depression and have fun, Captain!"

The good Captain Jonas Von Stockhausen received a letter wherein Luther advised many admonitions about how the Captain should and should not think (see chapter 7). In the same letter, Luther also gave advice about behavior. On November 27, 1532, Luther advised Von Stockhausen to say to the devil, "I must eat, drink, ride, go, or do this or that." Luther further advised, "Undertake to do anything else that you are able—whether play or something else."[103]

"Play away your depression, Maestro!"

Jerome Weller's brother, Matthias, was a talented enough musician to be organist at the cathedral in Freiberg, Saxony. Matthias experienced depression, much as Jerome did. In seemingly obvious advice, but advice not at all obvious to someone in the throes of depression, Luther advised Matthias to do what Matthias probably enjoyed doing more than anything.

> When you are sad, therefore, and when melancholy threatens to get the upper hand, say: "Arise! I must play a song unto the Lord on my regal [according to Tappert, the regal is a portable organ] (be it the *Te Deum audamus* or the *Benedictus*), for the Scriptures teach us that it pleases Him to hear a joyful song and the music of stringed instruments." Then begin striking the keys and singing in accompaniment, as David and Elisha did, until you're sad thoughts vanish. If the devil returns and plants worries and sad thoughts in your mind, resist him manfully and say, "Begone, devil! I must now play and sing unto my Lord Christ."[104]

Here again, Luther used the cognitive strategy of normalization to encourage healthy behavior, pointing out that playing music and singing was done by the fathers of faith.

APPLYING BEHAVIORAL PRINCIPLES

Luther's helpful advice regarding behavior to combat depression and anxiety is straightforward. His advice is commonsensical, and you can and should offer the same advice; it is advice given by mental health professionals. To start, evaluate a person's behavior, then enlighten him or her about the importance of behavior. Next, encourage and advise him or her to change his or her behavior.

Evaluate

When talking with someone who is depressed or anxious, he will likely not talk about avoiding others and cultivating solitude. Therefore, it is useful to ask him about his behavior. Ask him what he has been doing lately. In particular, ask him what he does regularly for fun. Do not be surprised if he asks what you mean. He might not recognize the word *fun*, or at least he won't be recently familiar with the notion. Simply repeat the question, "Fun. How often do you do things for fun?"

You may hear that he doesn't often do fun things. In this case, ask him what he used to do for fun. Again, it might take some time for him to recall and respond, but be persistent. Surely he used to do fun things! Surely he used to be fun! Alternatively, if he has an answer and mentions some fun activities, ask him both how often he does these things and how much he enjoys them. Do not assume he is not doing fun things. He might do fun things that depress him anyway. Alternatively, he might do fun things, but he might not do them often enough. He might mention things as fun but not actually find them that much fun. So follow up with other gentle questions, such as how often he does these activities and how much he enjoys doing them.

Some example questions might be:

- "What do you do for fun?"
- "What is the last thing you did that was fun?"
- "Are there things you used to enjoy doing that you do not do any longer?"

Do not allow anyone to tell you that they get their fun through social media. *Social media* is the most misleading term in the English language, with the possible exception of *funny pietist*. There is nothing social about social media. It is incredibly antisocial. If overused to the point of promoting solitude, it can be damaging to emotional health.

Insist that socialization is done face to face. Do not condemn social media, although there's much to condemn about it. We will have social media until the end of days. Research, though, clearly shows the damaging effects of social media when it starts to be substituted for face-to-face interactions. However, if social media does not take the place of face-to-face interactions, it is not particularly damaging to emotional well-being.

Enlighten

As appropriate, suggest to her that it is very important, as Luther said, to do fun things. Emphasize that doing fun things is the single most important thing someone can do for their mental health, which it is. You can perhaps say some version of the following:

- "Luther's advice to persons with depression and anxiety was to have fun."
- "Do you think people in heaven are isolated?"
- "Have you read about the importance of fellowship in the Bible?"

It will not likely be difficult to convince her of the advantage of doing fun things, but be patient as she might be reluctant to admit this. This might happen because she has guessed what happens if she admits that socializing and having fun are important.

Advise and Encourage

After getting a sense of what he does for fun or what he used to do for fun, and after getting at least a reluctant agreement that doing more things that he enjoys is a good idea, get him to commit to doing these activities. He has recognized how important it is for his mental well-being and has come to you for assistance. This is one of the most important things he can do. Ask the following:

- "What fun things can you commit to doing every week?"

- "What things that you used to enjoy can you do again?"
- "You sometimes do things for fun. Can you do them more?"

For couples in distress, simple behavioral strategies can be very helpful. It is not always the case that distress is because the husband and wife have ceased loving each other. It is often the case that they simply have forgotten to enjoy each other's company, which is how they were attracted to each other in the first place. Some simple suggestions to couples in distress include these:

- "Make your relationship a priority."
- "Set a weekly date night. Take turns deciding what to do each week."
- "Ban children from the room while you catch up on each other's day."

Socialization

The main behavioral goals to combat mental health problems are fun and socialization. They tend to go together. In pursuit of the goal of doing more fun things, encourage the person experiencing distress to recognize the importance of socialization.

Suggest that the first step is to reach out to friends. Friends are an important resource for these behavior strategies. Friends are a source of socialization and a source of fun. If she has been avoiding friends or turning down invitations, she is likely to be reluctant to reach out. She might think that her friends are angry or disappointed, which they might be. She will thus be embarrassed about the future conversation. Encourage her, using cognitive strategies, to rethink her choices. Remind her that her friends like her and would probably appreciate the opportunity to help her. Encourage her to ignore her thinking and associated feeling of potential embarrassment. Ask and suggest the following:

- "Who among your friends can you start to engage with?"

- Arrange specific events with friends. If certain friends prefer spontaneity, seek out other friends. Scheduling is important. Ask friends not to allow them to cancel.

- Confide her emotional struggles with her friends. If necessary, apologize for not responding or for canceling. Tell friends they could use their help in battling depression.

HEALTHY AND UNHEALTHY BEHAVIOR

For some reason, we don't have many examples of Luther advising a proper diet or exercise. Evidence and imagination suggest it is likely that Luther was a beloved companion to many. He enjoyed so many of life's pleasures, and he avidly sought them, probably in part to keep at bay his depression and anxiety. He knew the effects of stress on health, but we don't have evidence that the effects of diet, sleep, and exercise were known in his day.

Luther and Stress

Luther knew that his work habits caused him problems. He wrote that he had been working hard to Melanchthon on May 12, 1530, but that he was then overcome with stress. He wrote, "Suddenly the outward man collapsed, unable to sustain the fervor of the inner renewed man. I felt a loud buzzing and roaring, like thunder, in my head, and had I not stopped at once I would've fainted, and [then I] was useless for two days. The machine will do no more." He then advised his friend, "Take care of your health, and do not injure your head, as I have done. I shall request our friends to try to prevent you overstepping the limitations which your health demands; spare yourself, so that you may not be a self-murderer."[105]

Other Health Behaviors

In some letters, Luther complained about sleep, but mostly in reference to exhaustion. A man of his time, Luther would not have known that diet, sleep, and exercise were important to physical and emotional health (he often wrote, perhaps in jest, advising beer as a tonic). For much of human history, the issue regarding food has not been, "Is it healthy for me?" but rather, "Is there enough to keep me and my family from starving?" Needing to exercise because of sedentary jobs and the ease of getting from place to place by vehicle was not a commonplace problem. People were active to the point of exhaustion whether they wanted to be or not. Research has, however, revealed much about the importance of sleep, diet, and exercise to physical and emotional health.

Advice to Others Regarding Healthy Behaviors

Diet, exercise, stress, and sleep habits are not easy to change from unhealthy to healthy. Because of this, I will not spend much time advising about these topics. It is not my area of expertise, and advice is easily accessed. Evaluating healthy behaviors can be useful, though, and it might be good to encourage people to adopt healthier behaviors. All persons ought to follow this advice, but it is especially important for those with mental health problems. These persons are most at risk for unhealthy behavior. An effective way to convince someone to care for himself is to remind him that his capacity to care for others is compromised if he is not first caring for himself.

Regarding *exercise,* research demonstrates that it is very important to mental health. Regular exercise is effective in alleviating depression, anxiety, posttraumatic stress disorder, attention-deficit hyperactivity disorder, and other mental health problems.

Asking about exercise is somewhat fraught because of misunderstanding of what healthy exercise entails. Our society celebrates athletic ability, and many mistakenly think that exercise means hours of running a week, bodybuilding, or aerobics. In reality, recommendations entail moving one's body to get the heart rate above ninety beats per minute for about thirty minutes per day. Any activity that does this counts as exercise.

Sleep is important for health and especially for mental health. A person with significant mental health problems is likely to have sleep problems. Asking about sleep is as simple as saying, "How are you sleeping?" If it is an issue, encourage her to read about "sleep hygiene."

Ask if she *eats healthy* and if she thinks she should eat more healthy. It is not necessary to provide strategies for healthy eating. Such advice is readily available.

Socialization and fun are recreational activities essential for *dealing with stress*. Hobbies are also great for combating stress. By definition, these are things a person finds enjoyable. Hobbies are behavioral habits, and renewing an old hobby or pursuing a new hobby are wonderful ideas to alleviate emotional distress. Distracting and enjoyable, they often give a sense of accomplishment.

ALL THINGS NEEDFUL

Attending church is *extremely* important to mental health. Church is where people hear God declare, through the pastor, that their sins are forgiven. They receive the Sacrament. They are nourished in their faith by the company of fellow believers. More prosaically, but important to mental health, church is full of friendly people, the Body of Christ.

Chapter 9

Applying Luther's Advice

Therefore, my beloved brothers, be steadfast, immovable, always abounding in the work of the Lord, knowing that in the Lord your labor is not in vain. I Corinthians 15:58

This chapter has two parts. The first concerns how readers can help persons with mental health problems, either experienced personally or affecting someone close to them. Individual help is described as a "helpful conversation." The second part reviews "outreach strategies," which are things that churches can do to address stigma and be more open and welcoming to those experiencing mental health problems.

PRACTICAL AND INTERPERSONAL CONSIDERATIONS TO HELP INDIVIDUALS

Strategies for helping someone in emotional distress change his or her thinking or behavior were reviewed in chapters 7 and 8. These strategies can be implemented within the context of "helpful conversations." This chapter reviews the goals of a helpful conversation, then discusses essential or foundational characteristics of helpful conversations, as well as practical and interpersonal considerations. Conversations that lack these characteristics and considerations could result in persons feeling closed off to advice or consultation.

How Helpful Conversations Start

There are two ways a conversation might begin with someone distressed by a mental health problem. Luther's letters attest to both. Sometimes Luther wrote to someone with whom he had personal knowledge and familiarity. In the same way, a person distressed by a mental health problem will most likely come directly to you, seeking assistance and consolation. The only preparation necessary for these conversations is not being surprised that mental health problems exist in your church and not acting surprised that the person coming to you is experiencing mental health problems.

Other times, Luther wrote to someone after learning about his or her struggles from another person. In like manner, there will be times when you will be obliged to approach someone about a mental health concern. It might be that you become concerned, or it might happen that someone else talks to you about another person. In other words, you might need to initiate some helpful conversations.

Goals of a Helpful Conversation

Before reviewing the goals of a helpful conversation, let us be clear about what the goal is not. A helpful conversation does not solve someone's problems. That would be a wonderful thing to do, obviously, but it is very unlikely to be possible. Thinking that you must help solve someone's problems puts a great deal of pressure on you. It would make any reader hesitant to meet with someone in emotional distress. But the reality is that you cannot solve his problems. You cannot find him a better job, a faithful spouse, or a better group of friends. You cannot undo his trauma, nor give him brains that do not produce hallucinations, nor cure his child of autism, nor turn back time to give him a better childhood.

A helpful conversation is helpful when it addresses with compassion and kindness what the person is experiencing. Some things are fairly safe to assume the person is experiencing. First, the person is distraught, probably with a mix of depression and anxiety. Second, the person is confused. In particular, she may not understand why she feels this way. Or perhaps she does not know what to do about it. The reasons and even answers might be obvious to others but not to her. As a result, the person very likely thinks badly of herself and thinks others think badly of her as well. Third, the person is anxious about talking to you about her emotional distress. If she cannot understand herself, she might think you and others will surely find her weird and pathetic.

The goals of a helpful conversation follow from this. When you listen with kindness and express understanding of her distress, you can alleviate her confusion and her shame. She has most likely been sure, up until meeting you, that no one could understand her or would care. By striving to understand, you signal that their distress is okay. By expressing understanding, you communicate that she us understandable, not confusing.

This sounds like a large task, but it is not. The task is mostly, if not completely, accomplished by the simple kindness of meeting, listening, and offering comfort and consolation. At the most simple level, the simple kindness of setting aside your valuable time and listening to a person with a mental health problem will lessen her distress. It won't solve her problems, but she will feel less alone because you are standing with her in that distress.

In summary, listening with kindness and care, striving to understand, and offering simple words of comfort and consolation like Luther did will profoundly disrupt her sense of shame.

Emulate Luther's Manner

Emulating Luther is not always a great idea, but his manner of dealing with persons in emotional distress is worth copying.

Luther's Kindness

Tappert provides us with first-person observations of Luther's interpersonal style, as recorded by Conrad Cordatus. We learn that Luther was kind and friendly. He did not hesitate to ask anything.

> When he [Luther] approaches a sick man he converses with
> him in a very friendly way, bends down as close to him as he
> can with his whole body, and first inquires about his illness,
> what his ailment is, how long he has been sick, what physician
> he has called, and what kind of medicine he has been using.[106]

From letters he wrote, we also know that Luther was empathic, sympathetic, and patient. He labored to make others know that he cared and that he understood. He used his own experiences to inform this effort. He shared his own experiences so that others would not feel alone or strange. He experienced anxiety and depression, his life was under threat, he was in near-constant pain much of his last two decades of life, he had grieved the death of his children, he worried about the affection of his friends, and he wept at the death of his parents and friends. He was a man familiar with sorrow. He did not flinch from the grief, pain, and sorrows of others.

Luther's Steadfastness

If you are a worker in the Lord's vineyard, you know you should not shrink from or shirk obligations to brothers and sisters who are physically suffering. You would not do this in the face of medical problems or even in the face of death. Do not do that here. If you are not a pastor or other professional worker in the church, you, too, know you are supposed to love and serve your neighbor in every physical need. Be there also for those with mental health problems.

Be steadfast in applying and using the advantage you have that mental health professionals do not. You can assure those in mental and emotional distress that feeling depressed and anxious is not a sin. You can remind them of Christ's redeeming sacrifice, His forgiveness, and their salvation. Luther was not just steadfast. He was adamant in regard to matters of salvation. He said, essentially, "This you must believe!" Like Luther, be bold in this proclamation. Insist on the truth, but be patient with those who struggle to believe. Remember Luther's words of consolation to his pastor friend who fretted about his own doubts, "I thought it was only me!" Point out that Luther always stated that doubts were normal, expected, and a part of the Christian's life on earth. Tell the person that Luther practically invented a term, *Anfechtung*, for his own struggles with faith.

Luther's Hesitant Boldness

Luther did what many mental health professionals do. We know the connection between feeling and thinking, and we therefore often guess with confidence how a person with depression or anxiety is thinking. At the same time, we are cautious about sharing our guesses.

Presuming it did not concern matters of faith, about which he was resolute, Luther was likewise bold but cautious when guessing what another was thinking based on their expressed emotions. Luther had good empathy and an abundance of personal experience. He knew about negative thinking. He could not, however, simply point out the objective reality of the Bible and expect immediate results. Nor could he refer to observable behavior and trust that persons in distress understood what they were doing. Nor would he assert certainty about the way the person was thinking because only the person experiencing the mental health problems truly understands that distress.

He expressed this directly to Prince Joachim. In the letter dated May 23, 1534, before offering, "It is my opinion that Your Grace is reluctant to be merry," Luther starts with, "If I am mistaken in my judgment and have done Your Grace an injustice, I hope that Your Grace will be good enough to forgive me."[107]

Although, like Luther, we can be fairly certain what someone suffering from depression and anxiety is thinking, it is important to avoid making these assumptions with absolute certainty, as the person may find it offensive or objectionable. We can be pretty sure that these persons are thinking negatively about themselves, others, and relationships. But we can also be sure that they are not always aware of how they think. Luther gently but firmly encouraged people to think about their thinking, and so should you.

Practical Considerations

A helpful conversation should happen in *private*. Invite the person for a chat at church or request a visit to his or her home. Helpful conversations can happen over the phone or via virtual meetings, but they are best in person.

A helpful conversation needs *sufficient time*. It will take a while to listen to the story of a person's distress. I recommend between thirty and fifty minutes. At the beginning of the meeting, explain when the meeting will end so that the awkwardness of ending is made easier. Position a clock somewhere that you can see it easily when briefly glancing past the person. It can be awkward to have to look at one's watch or even worse, to look behind oneself to see what time it is. This body language communicates to the person that you are looking forward to the meeting being over. At the end, say something like, "I'm aware of the time." Say this with ten minutes left so that you can summarize what the person said and also summarize your counsel.

Pay careful attention to *physical space*. Having a desk between you and the other person might communicate that you are fearful of or repulsed by them. Arrange the chairs so that they are at a slight angle to each other, which makes it easier for either of you to briefly avert your gaze, which might be helpful when especially painful topics are discussed.

Finally, consider the issue of *confidentiality*. You should state that you will not share any information with others, but you should also state that confidentiality has its limits. Inform them of obligations to act after disclosures of child maltreatment or potential danger to self or others, even if that means breaking confidentiality.

Nonverbal Communication

Nonverbal communication occurs nonstop through facial expressions, posture and movement, and nonverbal utterances. People communicate their feelings especially through nonverbal communication. From this, we can guess what they are thinking. You easily know a loved one is anxious, angry, or sad, even though they say nothing. Consider how comforting a smile from a loved one can be when you are upset or how distressing to realize, by just a fleeting facial expression, that you hurt someone's feelings unintentionally.

If we become aware of nonverbal communication, we can be intentional about what we communicate to others and use it to our advantage in a helpful conversation.

Facial expressions can communicate understanding, a nonjudgmental attitude, and acceptance. A helpful facial expression is *relaxed* interest, which might lead to a small and gentle *smile* to match your compassionate attitude. *Nodding* one's head encouragingly is an extremely effective way to show someone in distress that you are striving to understand and that you want him or her to continue talking. Consistent *eye contact* communicates interest and concern.

An example of unintentional *body language* that might hurt the willingness of someone to keep talking is crossed arms. This signals to the other person that you are not open to what is being said. Instead, adopt an *open posture*. Stand or sit with your *back straight* and your *head held upright* or at a slight angle. A powerful expression of interest is to *lean in a bit*.

Nonverbal utterances encourage someone to continue speaking. They include simple commiserative sounds, such as "right," "yes," and "um hm." They are powerful signals to the other person to keep talking. These come naturally to some, but anyone can develop the habit.

Active Listening and Empathy

Many persons in emotional distress do not understand why they are distressed. They know they have experienced upsetting events, but they tell themselves that the events are not worth this level of turmoil. The distress might be a mystery because negative thoughts have fallen out of awareness and unhealthy behaviors, such as isolation, have become habitual. As a result, they might be reluctant to discuss their distress. Also, they likely feel ashamed of their distress.

Simply discussing the distress can help immensely. During the discussion, you can show that you understand and accept it. This might not result in less confusion and will not cause the distress to disappear. It will, however, ease the distress by helping the person realize it is not strange, embarrassing, or shameful. To get the person to talk openly, utilize *active listening*. To communicate that his or her distress is understandable, utilize *empathy*.

Active Listening

Active listening entails verbal behaviors by the listener that encourage the other person to continue talking, expand on topics, and explore deeper. It helps the speaker realize she did the right thing confiding in you.

Reflective listening is sometimes called verbal mirroring. It is simply repeating back to the speaker his own words, perhaps paraphrasing slightly. The simple technique is surprisingly effective. It is particularly useful early in a conversation when you are uncertain about what is being discussed and what else to say. Reflection is almost word-for-word. For example:

- Speaker: "I felt so ashamed and alone."
- Listener: "You felt ashamed. You felt isolated."

✳

▦ Speaker: "You must think I am so strange."

▦ Listener: "You worry that others think you are strange."

Closed questions have explicit and discrete answers. They are used to fill in details. For example, someone describes their family, and you might ask, "How old are your kids?" Or if someone says he or she dislikes his or her job, you ask, "How long have you worked there?" Closed questions are useful for details and demonstrate that the listener is engaged and interested.

Open-ended questions require the speaker to elaborate. They are useful to prompt further description. For example, if someone describes his family to you, you might ask, "How did you and your wife meet?" Or if someone says he or she dislikes his or her job, you might ask, "What are some of the things you dislike the most?" Responses require elaboration. *Gentle commands* are similar. They are polite requests for elaboration, such as, "Tell me how you and your wife met," and, "Tell me the parts of your job you dislike the most."

Paraphrasing is a type of reflection. It entails repeating what the person said in a different way, demonstrating that you understand. Paraphrasing allows the speaker to reflect on the content of what he or she just said to you, and they might then correct a misunderstanding or provide further information. Examples of paraphrasing include:

▦ Speaker: "I was very upset!"

▦ Listener: "You felt angry."

▦ Speaker: "I was not so much angry as sad."

✳

▦ Speaker: "I feel like no one respects me."

▦ Listener: "You think others don't appreciate your expertise."

Speaker: "They treat me like I don't know what I'm doing."

Summarizing is a longer version of paraphrasing. Summary is done at the end of a conversation or at the turning point to another topic. Summarizing what was said shows the person that he or she has been heard and understood. Like paraphrasing, summaries can prompt a speaker to correct a misunderstanding or to clarify further. An accurate summary may elicit profound relief in the person. Summary statements often start with, "So let me see if I understand what you have been saying . . ." or, "Let me check to make sure I'm following you . . ."

Empathy

Empathy means understanding and accepting how a person thinks and feels with no judgment or evaluation of his or her thoughts and feelings. It is not feeling what the speaker is feeling; that is sympathy. It is not agreeing with what the speaker is thinking, which might be impossible and unwise. For example, if a woman tells you she thinks her husband is cheating on her, you can empathize with what she is thinking, but it would be unwise to agree with her thinking. Empathy is understanding, even if you do not quite agree or are unsure that what a person is thinking is accurate.

Empathizing with someone's emotions is especially important; its effect on a person coping with mental health problems is profoundly helpful. To empathize with a person in distress means standing as a nonjudgmental, kind, and unflinching witness to his or her pain.

Empathy encourages people to realize their emotions or thoughts, while unpleasant, distressing, and confusing are understandable. If you understand what the person is going through, then by definition, what the person is going through is understandable. Moreover, it will suggest that others might also understand.

Empathy starts as an internal cognition on the part of the listener, but it must be communicated to the speaker to be helpful. To do this, use the techniques of active listening. Reflection of emotional content is effective, as is paraphrasing into synonyms of emotions being expressed. Some examples of using active listening in empathy are:

- Speaker: "I felt so depressed when that happened."
- Listener: "When that happened, you felt very sad."

✳

- Speaker: "It was so confusing to hear that."
- Listener: "You were unsure and baffled by what you were hearing."

✳

- Speaker: [The speaker describes a long history of arguing with her elderly parents and says she is confused, upset, and also feeling guilty.]
- Listener: "The situation is causing all sorts of emotions. You feel bad about being upset. You are confused as to what they are trying to do. It's a mix of feelings."

Behaviors That Derail a Helpful Conversation

These are some behaviors that should be avoided, as they detract from a helpful conversation.

Interrupting is bad manners in any conversation, but it is antithetical to a helpful conversation. It indicates impatience, disinterest, a desire to dominate the conversation, and a lack of understanding of the speaker's pain.

"Why" questions tend to make people feel they have done something wrong or that the listener is being critical. To make someone feel defensive, ask, "Why did you feel like that?" or "Why did you do that?"

Quick reassurance and *quick advice* are popular behavior during discussions, especially for men who see every problem as an opportunity to find a solution. *Quick reassurance* communicates to the person that what he is concerned about is trivial. Examples include, "Don't worry about that," "Everyone gets sad sometimes," or "Try to get over it."

Quick advice communicates that the listener thinks the speaker is unable to come up with the obvious solution to an easy problem. Advice is not a bad thing, but quick advice before listening and empathizing is never a good thing. Quick advice examples often include the word *should*, such as "You should quit," "You should talk to your spouse more," and "You should try yoga, meditation, medication, or some similar strategy that I think will work for everyone." These might be meant to make the person feel better, but they do not. They communicate a desire to be done with the conversation.

Insistence on disclosure is antithetical to a helpful conversation. It is essential to recognize and to respect when a discussion has reached a topic that makes the speaker uncomfortable. In therapy, after months of work together, it is usually true that "nothing is off limits." But this takes a long time to establish such trust. Not respecting someone's need for discretion communicates to the person in distress that the listener does not understand his or her discomfort or, worse, doesn't care.

Address Stigma Immediately and Directly

Mary came to church on crutches. Everyone asked what happened, sympathized about her recent knee surgery, and asked how recovery was going. Martha came to church after several weeks of missing church. When she said she was hospitalized for depression for a month, most looked uncomfortable, said, "Good to see you again," and walked away as soon as they could.

Different Reactions

In your experience, does this sound about right? It surely would sound familiar to people in emotional distress. Reactions to physical hurt are predictable. If we tell someone we are confronting an illness, we are confident that he or she will not think negatively about us, will not feel uncomfortable, will react with sympathy, and might even ask about treatment. Reactions to emotional hurt are also predictable, but they are not as satisfying. If we tell someone we have depression, anxiety, a substance use problem, or another issue, most persons are unsure what to say.

Society's agreed-upon "knowledge" about mental illness—that persons with mental health problems are strange and dangerous—affects all of us. Since we do not talk much about mental health problems as a society, we are not exposed to accurate or corrective information. We all know many with mental health problems, but we do not necessarily know who they are and are therefore not able to realize persons with mental health problems are just like everyone else. When hearing about mental health problems, persons do not know what they should think, they feel uncomfortable, and they might act as if something shameful has just been disclosed.

Now armed with the information in this book, you will hopefully not do that. When someone tells you about their emotional hurt, express empathy, acceptance, and understanding: "Oh, too bad. That's sounds difficult. A lot of people go through that." As you would with medical health problems, ask about treatment: "Are you in treatment? How is it going?"

It might be beneficial to the person in emotional distress to hear you explicitly acknowledge the stigma they have likely experienced.

Discuss Stigma

Discussing the stigma attached to mental health problems takes sensitivity and may not be a topic broached at all. But if there are hints that someone has experienced stigma about his or her mental health problem, consider that an invitation to talk about it. For example, someone might say, "My sister hates hearing about my struggle with depression. She does not know how to deal with it." You might respond by acknowledging the pain of such a reaction. You might say, "It sounds like she doesn't really understand depression. So many people don't. It is treated by some as weird or shameful." Denounce such stigmatizing attitudes, feelings, and behaviors, perhaps by saying, "It is too bad people are so uninformed and can feel so negatively and act so badly toward those who are struggling."

Helping Families

Family members of persons with mental illness also face burdens related to stigma and related to the struggle with the illness. Like the individuals themselves, family members can use a kind word and perhaps help with regard to the way they are thinking and behaving.

Burdens

As noted earlier, family members and caregivers of those with mental health problems are most stressed when the person has an SPMI. These illnesses are, by definition, serious and long-lasting. They can vary in severity from week to week and month to month, making them somewhat unpredictable, which is particularly stressful. Someone doing well can relapse into serious symptoms, even if they are compliant with treatment.

The burden applies to some extent to all mental illnesses. Any mental illness will cause concern and heartache in their family members. It is terrible to watch a husband experience depression or to see a daughter traumatized. These illnesses will hopefully resolve, but they can last a long time and be taxing on those who love them.

Family members and caregivers need empathy. They need others to acknowledge their pain and stand with them in their sorrow. They need encouragement and kindness. Keep in mind that they might hesitate to mention the burdens they carry. Some take the attitude of, *I am not the one with the illness, so I should not complain.* Show that you understand, which will encourage them to talk.

Emotions and Thoughts

Family members and caregivers experience a wide range of emotions. Constant caregiving of a person with a mental health problem can be exhausting. When someone does not get better, it can lead to frustration, sadness, and even anger.

When a caregiver experiences such emotions, he might think about his emotions and find them to be flawed or even sinful. He might think negatively about his negative emotions. This will cause him to feel guilty because of his anger, frustration, and occasional impatience. Many will feel terrible because they sometimes resent what God has given them. They might think, *I should not feel this way,* or, *I should accept willingly.*

If you realize that a person is thinking this way about a loved one's illness, encourage him to be more kind in how he thinks about himself. Encourage him not to compound his negative feelings with guilt. Remind him that unremitting stress will cause occasional negative emotions. Help him think better of himself, even if he occasionally feels sad and stressed. Point out their actual behavior to them so that he or she can better realize it. Observe aloud that his or her behavior has been loving and kind, even when upset. Comment on how strong he has acted and how obviously he loves the person with the mental health problem. If needed, remind him that God is tough and can handle his anger. Say, "Nothing will stop His love for you."

It is important not to assume, however. Realize that family members and caregivers can have many positive emotions about the person in their care. Directly caring for someone in great need, they likely frequently experience compassion, sympathy, and love from the person for whom they care and from others.

Courtesy Stigma

Courtesy stigma entails the negative thoughts, feelings, and behaviors directed at the family members of persons with mental health problems. As with the individual in distress, discussing stigma with family members and caregivers might be helpful. It would be empathic to their pain and could show that you understand what they are experiencing even if they do not bring it up. You can broach the topic by saying, "This is a tough situation for you. I know that it can be made even tougher by how some people think about these things. Some people are not especially understanding or kind." If they take the opening and want to talk further, do so.

The theology of glory offers a special, vicious, and evil stigma to family members. This false ideology says that mental health problems are the result of inadequate faith. Thus, any child or family member who has a mental health problem can be wrongly labeled as having fallen away from the faith. This is an odious, repugnant, and demonic thing to think and to say, but many think it, and some say it. Many families have heard or experienced some version of this. They might be hesitant to bring up this terrible experience out of fear that you might believe the same. Thus, if it seems needed, bring their experiences into the light. Acknowledge that they have experienced such evil so that it can be discussed and addressed. Either lament with them the awfulness of the thinking or, if necessary, correct their thinking. Encourage them to understand that faith has nothing to do with mental illness. Explicitly reject the notion that one determines the other. If you are not a pastor, encourage people experiencing courtesy stigma to see their pastor for further instruction and consolation in this regard.

Thinking and Emotions

Thoughts of self-blame are consistent with society's stigmatizing attitudes toward mental illness. Society does often attribute such problems to weakness and badness. Explicitly and forcefully discredit such notions.

Acknowledge that this is what many believe, but assert with confidence and authority that scientists have shown these ideas to be wrong. Confirm to them that you do not believe such ideas and that they should not either.

Self-Care Behaviors

As appropriate, emphasize that self-care is important. Encourage family members and caregivers to seek social support through regular conversations with others in similar situations. Encourage them to get out and have fun when they can. Encourage family members and caregivers to come to church. They need to hear the Gospel. They need God's word of comfort. They need to know that their fellow church members love them.

CHURCHWIDE STRATEGIES

A large survey asked both clergy and church members about mental health issues.[108] The survey compared clergy responses with the responses of those with mental illness. Most clergy said they wanted to help parishioners with mental illness, but few clergy said that they incorporated messages about mental illness into Bible studies, sermons, or meetings.

The survey revealed that those with mental illness noticed. Persons and families said they wished their church talked more openly about mental illness, but most said that their church did not. This experience made them feel ignored, invisible, and unseen. In other words, they experienced stigma at their church.

Sometimes stigma is more than ignorance and ignoring. It can be much more explicit. The Rev. Dr. Matthew C. Harrison, president of The Lutheran Church—Missouri Synod, wrote, "Unbelievably—I've heard this many, many times—there are clergy who are convinced that strong faith will exclude depression. . . . I've also heard it argued that faith, and seeking remedy for depression in the means of grace, should exclude the need for medical diagnosis and treatment."[109]

What about Your Church?

Do you think persons with mental health problems experience stigma at your church? We all hope not, but it would be better to know for sure. Below are some questions to consider.

Is there laughter and scorn about mental health problems? Do the one in five persons with mental illness in your church feel welcome? Do they feel seen? Do their families feel welcome, comforted, and reassured? Can you point to things that your church does to make them feel welcome? Does your church do things to show that their pain is known? Is there preaching on the theology of glory with regard to the problem?

Do members of your church think that mental health problems are voluntary, shameful, and selfish? Do they believe that they are a sign of weakness? Do they believe that they are an indication of weak faith? If you do not know these things, you should find out.

Even without knowing who they are, there are many ways that churches, pastors, and members can demonstrate that they welcome and have compassion for persons struggling.

Uncover What Has Been Hidden for Too Long

Communicate to persons with mental health problems that the church knows they are present. This invites them to show themselves, which will enable you to help.

Some acts are simple:

- Include *petitions* in the prayers for those in emotional distress.
- Include *bulletin announcements* about the availability of local mental health resources.
- Dedicate a *Bible study* to mental health problems. Perhaps study Luther's letters.

Some actions take courage:

▨ Insist upon both *sense and sensitivity* about mental illness.

▨ *Admonish and educate* anyone who ridicules mental health problems as trivial, pathetic, or frightening.

▨ *Confront* anyone telling inappropriate jokes, repeating unkind stories, or using derogatory language to describe mental illness.

Some actions take some effort:

▨ Develop in yourself and encourage in others the habit of using *people-first language* to refer to persons with mental illness, such as "a person with schizophrenia" instead of "a schizophrenic."

▨ Establish a board or task force to evaluate the mental health needs of the congregation. It could be comprised of persons with relevant experience or expertise. It could be tasked with implementing strategies to ensure that persons with mental health problems *feel welcome* at church. It could do regular surveys of persons in the church. The board could report what persons with mental health problems think about the church. The board or task force should report to and be part of the leadership of the church.

▨ Invite a *speaker* or host a *seminar* about mental illness and its treatment. Mental health clinics, training programs, and individual providers are usually willing to do this. I strongly recommend seeking someone who presents on the topic regularly.

▨ Provide training for elders, ushers, and greeters to be welcoming and supportive of persons with mental illness.

All such activities—whether weekly or occasional, whether large or small—declare forthrightly that your church is not afraid of mental illness, is not ashamed of those that struggle with one, and is open to talking about those struggles. These actions will demonstrate to those in distress, "We know you are here, and we welcome you with love."

Call Out and Condemn the Depredations of the Theology of Glory

The theology of glory is poison to all Christians, but it is perhaps most injurious to those with mental health problems. Its basic message is, "Emotional distress is due to weak faith." As Luther did, continually condemn this heretical teaching. As Luther did, console those in distress by reminding them that Christ bore all sins on the cross. Help them understand that being a Christian does not protect them from mental health problems. As common as this corrupt theology is, there are many opportunities to condemn and attack it.

Preach and teach that whether we feel good or not, Christ has won our victory and our freedom from sin, death, and hell. "In the world you will have tribulation. But take heart; I have overcome the world" (John 16:33). "So if the Son sets you free, you will be free indeed" (John 8:36). If you are a pastor, preach Christ crucified in all its comfort and consolation. If you are not a pastor, speak the Gospel of Christ crucified in whatever vocation God has placed you.

I encourage readers to consider the issue of outreach with the seriousness that Luther treated it. If persons with mental health problems and their families do not feel welcome at church, they will not hear the Word of God and they may walk away from the faith.

In contrast, outreach to persons and families struggling with mental illness can make them feel welcome. The comfort and consolation they receive about their distress will bring them back to hear God's message. As

Paul instructs us, "So faith comes from hearing, and hearing through the word of Christ" (Romans 10:17). Even if they do not disclose to anyone that they struggle with mental health problems, persons and families will greatly appreciate that the pastor and their fellow members know they exist and know that they are present.

Chapter 10

Helping versus Referring

Dear friend, I pray that you may enjoy good health and that all may go well with you, even as your soul is getting along well. 3 John 2

This chapter discusses evaluating mental health problems to determine severity and need.

DETERMINING THE SEVERITY OF MENTAL HEALTH PROBLEMS: WHO NEEDS REFERRAL?

In health care, during the initial evaluation, professionals sometimes realize that standard care will not be sufficient and immediate attention is needed. Readers should do something similar in their initial helpful conversation with a person experiencing mental health problems. In this conversation, they should decide whether a few more meetings to provide the advice discussed previously will likely be sufficient or, alternatively, that a referral to treatment by a professional is needed. This decision will be based on the severity of the problem. Mental health lies on a continuum, and serious problems require referral.

The following will help you evaluate the seriousness of a person's problems. Most important, however, is the rule of thumb every professional follows: trust your gut. Even if you cannot recognize what thoughts or impressions are driving the feeling, if your gut tells you that a person needs more than you can give—if you are uncomfortable at the prospect of trying to help—trust this feeling. Refer to a professional.

Indicators of Severity

There are several severity indicators. All can be queried directly.

Sudden and substantial changes in how a person feels, thinks, or behaves suggest that something has happened recently. There might have been a recent trauma or unpleasant life event. Sudden-onset depression and anxiety might be serious issues. Notable changes how a person thinks and behaves, such as excessive energy or odd behavior, are also serious. These changes might indicate undiagnosed schizophrenia or bipolar disorder or perhaps a reemergence of symptoms previously controlled. Sudden-onset problems might be due to recent or exacerbated substance abuse. Such changes also occur with medical problems. In all instances, provide a referral to a medical professional who can refer to a mental health professional as needed.

Emotional distress related to a *recent and severe trauma* is serious. These include serious injury or the unexpected death of a loved one. Traumas in the past are not as concerning, but they must be evaluated. If a past trauma is still seriously bothering her, especially if she has never sought help for it, she likely needs treatment from a mental health professional.

The *intensity of distress* is an important indicator of seriousness. It is axiomatic that someone who says she is sad is less seriously depressed than someone who cannot stop crying. Serious distress will be observable and evident.

The *duration of the problem* is another indication of severity. Longstanding, intense distress is serious. She might be experiencing a never-treated, persistent illness, such as major depression. Some never seek treatment because they get desensitized to their own distress. Alternatively, someone with longstanding distress might have received it in the past.

The *impact of the problem on roles and relationships* is another indicator of severity. Any mental health issues that cause problems with family or loved ones or with work or school performance are serious and should probably be referred. When evaluating the impact on roles and relationships, bear in mind that most persons underestimate this. Consulting with loved ones might be a good idea.

Suicidal Ideation and Intent

Thoughts about *suicide* are an indicator of a serious problem. Persons with mental illness are at higher risk of suicide attempts and completions than those without mental illness. Risk increases with the level of distress and impairment. This is especially true for persons with depression, bipolar disorder, schizophrenia, and substance use disorders.

The distinction between suicidal ideation and suicidal intent is important. Most persons think about their own deaths at times. Death ideation can be unsettling, especially when it occurs in a young person, but it is not necessarily a concern. Thinking about suicide is much more serious, especially if it is the result of emotional distress. Suicidal ideation is a serious symptom of depression, and the person needs referral to a mental health professional.

Suicide intent is the expressed intention to harm or kill oneself. It must be acted upon immediately. Anyone expressing suicide intent should be taken for immediate care. In extreme situations, immediate help from public safety personnel may be required.

Questions to Determine Severity

It is important to ask about severity. If you do not, the person will not tell you. The following questions might be used to determine severity.

Intensity of Distress

"How intense is the depression or anxiety you are experiencing?"

"Is this situation unbearable?"

"On a scale of one to ten, how bad is it?"

Duration

"When did all of this start?"

"How long has this been going on?"

"Is this recent, or has this been going on for a while?"

Trauma

"Was there something bad that happened to cause this?"

"Did this start because something happened?"

"Did this come out of nowhere, or did something seem to cause this?"

Suicidal Ideation and Intent

These questions should be asked in a matter-of-fact, concerned, and straightforward way.

"Sometimes when people are feeling distressed, they have thoughts of hurting themselves. Have you had any thoughts like that?"

"Have you been thinking that you wanted to hurt yourself?"

"Have you thought about hurting yourself or killing yourself?"

OFFERING HELP

This book familiarizes readers with advice about the thinking and behavior that Luther and mental health professionals dispense to help persons in emotional distress. There are important caveats about offering help. These should be understood at the outset by both you and the other person.

It will be short-term. If you think you should offer to help, understand that you are able to meet only for a limited number of time. If someone needs more help than can be given in three or four meetings, a referral to a professional is needed.

It will be oriented to changing thinking and behavior. Luther advised people to change. Your advice should likely entail focused guidance on how people can change their thinking and behavior.

To summarize chapter 7, regarding thinking, you should advise:

- "Your thinking is affecting how you feel and what you do."
- "Become more aware of what you are thinking."
- "Realize and accept that your thinking is often wrong."
- "Change your thinking to be more accurate, if you can."
- "If you cannot change it, ignore your thinking because it is untrue."

To summarize chapter 8, regarding behavior, you should advise:

- "Realize that your behavior is unhealthy."
- "For the sake of your mental health, do fun things."
- "For the sake of your mental health, go out with others."
- "Come to church every Sunday, whether you feel like it or not."
- "Improve your sleep habits, eat more nutritiously, and get more exercise."

MAKING A REFERRAL FOR PROFESSIONAL HELP

After a helpful conversation and determining the severity, you may realize that the person needs professional help.

Working within Competence versus Pressure to Help

During emotional distress, Christians often turn to their church. Their church is the source of much comfort and the site of important life events, such as the Baptisms of their children and the funerals of their parents.

Many want to be counseled by their pastor due to comfort and familiarity. Some view him as the most appropriate and competent resource, others as convenient (and free). Some will presume their pastor cannot refuse a request for help and might be resistant to a referral. They might be appalled that you think they are crazy for needing professional help. They will argue you know them better than a therapist and express discomfort at the prospect of "talking to a stranger."

Some pastors make similar mistakes in thinking. Some assume they are in the best position to help because of familiarity with the person or family. Some think of themselves as the only option if someone expresses disdain or discomfort regarding the mental health profession.

Yet how silly these ideas would be with other illnesses, such as heart disease, cancer, or serious injury. Imagine someone with cancer saying, "Pastor, I prefer you to a medical professional; you know me better, and I feel awkward talking to a stranger." Even more foolish would be the reader agreeing with that sentiment. Not providing a referral would be an abrogation of the responsibility to encourage parishioners to act responsibly with regard to their health. In addition, you cannot see everyone in your church—one in five persons—who needs such assistance. You cannot dedicate the time needed to help someone with a serious mental health problem, meaning weekly visits for several months or years. Fortunately, it is not necessary, for God has provided us with competent health care providers.

Encourage Treatment Seeking

Encourage persons experiencing mental health problems to seek treatment by expressing concern, pointing out the need for professional help, addressing stigma, and providing explicit guidance.

After listening via a helpful conversation, *communicate loving concern* about the person. Provide observations and repeat things that were discussed. Express concern about his or her behavior, feelings, or thinking.

Say, "This is very serious, and I am glad we are talking about it. However, this is more than I am competent to help with."

Psychoeducation is very important when referring. Many persons with mental health problems fail to recognize what is happening. If it seems evident, offer a guess as to which mental illness might be afflicting them, such as, "It seems to me that you are experiencing fairly substantial depression." Inform the person that mental illness is extremely common, both now, in the past, and in the Bible. Say treatment is effective and that refusing treatment is nonsensical.

Educate about what mental health professionals do and correct any misunderstanding. Many have incorrect information about providers of mental health care. Myths include ideas such as these:

- Counseling is "only talking," so it cannot possibly help.
- Mental health professionals can force patients to take medications.
- Medications will change who they are.
- Seeking mental health care is shameful and proof that you are crazy.
- Christians with strong enough faith do not need mental health professionals.

As needed, *address stigmatizing thoughts* and feelings of shame. Point out that no one wants to have a mental illness. Explain that a person's mental health problems are not due to weakness or badness. Insist that neither medical nor mental illness indicates a lack of faith. God understands that until Christ comes again, we will all live in an imperfect world. God does not punish sins by afflicting someone with mental health problems. Christ came to forgive our sins and take the punishment for our sins upon Himself so we do not have to suffer in eternity. When addressing mental health problems, talk about other individuals, without naming them, who have benefited from mental health care. Perhaps give examples of persons who have benefited from your own family or other church members.

Compliment the person on his or her willingness to talk with you. Point out that it seemed helpful that he did so, and this is a "good start." *Strongly encourage him to continue* to talk with a mental health professional with the expertise necessary to help. God has given us health professionals to perform the sacred duty of helping persons like them. State explicitly that you have confidence in mental health treatment and that you believe the person would benefit from it.

As appropriate, *strive to overcome resistance* by discussing the difference between how a person's life is currently and how he thought it would be. Empathize with his desire to be a good spouse, parent, friend, and worker, and point out that the way he is thinking and behaving is preventing him from doing as well as he wants to be doing.

There are *tangible obstacles* to treatment, such as availability of services, cost, insurance problems, and other access issues. Encourage the person to work through these issues, but do not attempt to work through the issues for him or her. Obstacles might actually be insurmountable, but they more likely only seem so since depression and anxiety lead to pessimistic thinking.

Be sure the person understands that it is your obligation—and his obligation—to see that he gets appropriate care. Assure the person that you are not referring out of embarrassment or discomfort. Tell him you intend to stay involved to provide spiritual counsel and consolation during his distress, just as you do with persons who have other illnesses.

DOMESTIC ABUSE MUST BE REFERRED

Domestic abuse is intentional acts of violence, threats, and control done by one person to another to intimidate and control the other person. Situations of domestic abuse are fraught with danger and risk, and the overarching concern is safety. Since an abuser dominates and controls a victim, when a victim tells someone else about experiences of abuse, it is inherently dangerous to him or her. If the issue comes up during a helpful conversation, discretion is necessary.

Disclosures about abuse will most certainly come as a surprise, and these disclosures will shock and upset you. Do *not allow emotions to dictate your behavior.* Do not confront someone you suspect of abuse. Do not even broach the topic. This could endanger the victim and his or her children. Do nothing immediately. If there is immediate danger to the victim or to children, contact public safety.

Rein in surprise and shock. Strive to be *nonjudgmental, kind, empathic, and supportive.* Respond with calm concern. Tell him or her you are very sorry about his or her experience. If appropriate, state that abuse is always wrong, illegal, and condemned by God.

State outright that the abuse has to end. Say you want to help him or her but are unable to do so. Discuss the paramount importance of safety. Say that the best, safest thing to do is to obtain professional assistance.

Refer the person to experts who have the expertise to help safely. Advise the victim of the importance of being cautious to not alert the abuser when reaching out to resources. Numerous national and state resources have 24/7 availability for consultation with victims.

Explicitly state that you will not be communicating with the abuser about what was said. To do so would drastically increase the likelihood of further abuse to a victim, so this should never be done. Nonetheless, the victim is likely to be anxious about this, so such reassurance will be welcome.

Both mental health professionals and clergy are often approached by victims or even perpetrators of abuse with a request for marital counseling. This is absolutely and unequivocally a bad idea. Domestic abuse is not a marital issue. It is one person abusing another. Doing marital counseling in an attempt to end domestic abuse assures that the abuse will continue.

PRACTICE DISCERNMENT WHEN SEEKING A MENTAL HEALTH PROVIDER

In a talk at the table recorded by Anthony Lauterbach in July 1538, when Luther was regularly experiencing health problems, he commented on a letter he had received from the elector of Saxony. The letter contained sympathetic words to Luther about his illness, but it also suggested that Luther was perhaps impatient with treatments. In response, Luther both commended and complained about physicians and their ministrations, sometimes with bitter sarcasm. But he also demonstrated great discernment.

It is true that the regimen prescribed by physicians should not be despised. But many physicians are so rash that they prescribe for the sick without discrimination. A new cemetery must be provided for them. On the other hand, others are too timid and undecided. They are uncertain about the illness and say, "Diagnosis is difficult, the weather is treacherous, the disease is acute," and they make the patient impatient with their many doubts.[110]

Luther seemed to be acknowledging his own impatience, but surely he had a point. And he wanted to make sure that his objective discernment and his subsequent opinion were not causing either hurt feelings or misunderstanding. He wanted no one to think he was not approving of physicians who themselves were discerning and careful. Also note the reference to Galenic theory about humors (vapors).

I have nothing but praise for the physicians who adhere closely to their principles. But they should not take it amiss if I cannot always agree with them, for they wish to make a fixed star out of me when I am a roving planet. . . . Our bodies contain many mysterious vapors and internal and invisible organs, there are also various and unexpected dangers; our bodies can go to pieces in an hour. Therefore, a physician must be humble.[III]

Finding Mental Health Professionals

Readers should practice discernment when referring to mental health professionals. You may be asked to provide the name of a mental health professional that you trust. This can be difficult for several reasons. The main issues are likely to be location and availability. Your preferred counselor might be far away or might have a full practice. Another issue is payment. Most seeking health care want insurance to help with the cost, and someone you might prefer might not take their insurance.

Accordingly, when you suggest someone see a professional, provide guidance on proper qualifications as follows. Unlike medical care, most mental health professionals make their own appointments. Thus, a phone call with a potential provider to schedule a meeting gives you an opportunity to ask questions so that you can be certain about his or her qualifications.

Seek only *licensed mental health professionals*. Licensure is based on graduate school education, a minimal level of experience, and demonstrated competence.

Seek someone with *relevant competence*. The main distinction in competence is whether someone works only with adults or also sees children. Other distinctions are special expertise in certain disorders. In my experience, those who claim competence to see everyone—all age groups, any problem or issue—are not likely to be especially competent with anyone.

Seek someone who explicitly recognizes the importance of *religious beliefs*. When calling for an appointment, seek assurance that the counselor respects religion. Even better is the counselor who will encourage clients to consult their pastor about any religious issue. It is not that a mental health professional should never ask a patient about religious beliefs. Given its importance to understanding a person, it would be good if he or she did so. Faith, however, should never be a focus of intervention. Many mental health professionals endorse antinomian ideology. They know that emotional distress is due to thinking. Thus, if thinking *I am a sinner* makes a person feel bad, then the thought must be wrong. Fortunately or not, most mental health professionals simply ignore the religious beliefs of patients.

Online counseling is becoming much more commonplace. It might be a good option, especially for persons in areas with a scarcity of mental health professionals. However, an initial consultation about their competence and their attitudes toward religion is even more important, as more and more providers work for corporations and do not schedule their own appointments. The first online meeting should cover these issues.

On Christian Counseling

You do not want a mental health professional discussing issues of faith with your parishioner. That is his or her pastor's responsibility. Christian counselors, though, have become major providers of mental health services, and a parishioner will likely express an inclination to seek out one.

The American Association of Christian Counselors counts almost fifty thousand members. Most are Bible-believing Baptists, Calvinists, or Pentecostals. But few are confessional Lutherans.[112]

Before referring to a Christian counselor, one should ask her, "What does that mean?" She might be a Christian who is a counselor. More likely, someone who says she is a Christian counselor is explicitly stating that she thinks it is legitimate and even beneficial to integrate religious beliefs into counseling. A Christian counselor might use prayer, religious readings, meditation, and explicit instructions. This raises some concerns.

First, many Christians, including Christian counselors, believe that all faiths are in essence the same, with only unimportant or surface-level differences. Second, any faith-based work in therapy will likely be congruent with the counselor's conception of proper Christian theology. Some will assert that they engage in advice only within the confines of the patient's faith. They might thus claim to understand of all Christian faiths, so they can adjust advice accordingly. Neither claim is believable. Of greatest concern, the counselor might strive to use the person's faith to try to make the person feel better. Toward this end, some may openly challenge their patients' religious beliefs and encourage them to change for the betterment of their mental health.

If someone insists on seeing a Christian counselor, be sure that she is willing to state that she ask about her client's faith, are respectful of that faith, and will refer back to her client's pastor in issues of faith.

Notes

1   For more information, see Stephen M. Saunders, *A Christian Guide to Mental Illness*, 2 vols. (Waukesha, WI: Northwestern Publishing House, 2009, 2012).

2   Theodore G. Tappert, ed. and trans., *Luther: Letters of Spritual Counsel* (Louisville: Wesminster Press, 1955), 82.

3   Tappert, *Luther*, 83.

4   Tappert, *Luther*, 83.

5   Tappert, *Luther*, 82.

6   Tappert, *Luther*, 85.

7   Tappert, *Luther*, 89.

8   Tappert, *Luther*, 89.

9   Tappert, *Luther*, 102.

10   Tappert, *Luther*, 93.

11   Tappert, *Luther*, 110.

12   Tappert, *Luther*, 110–11.

13   Tappert, *Luther*, 115.

14   Tappert, *Luther*, 116.

15   Tappert, *Luther*, 96.

16   "Statistics," National Institute of Mental Health (website), accessed March 13, 2023, https://www.nimh.nih.gov/health/statistics.

17   "Quick Facts and Statistics about Mental Health," Mental Health America (website), accessed March 13, 2023, mhanational.org /mentalhealthfacts.

18   "Prevalence of Any Mental Disorder among Adolescents," National Institute of Mental Health (website), accessed March 13, 2023, nimh .nih.gov/health/statistics/mental-illness#part_2632.

19   "Adverse Childhood Experiences," Centers for Disease Control and Prevention (website), accessed March 13, 2023, cdc.gov/vitalsigns /aces/index.html.

20 "The National Intimate Partner and Sexual Violence Survey," Centers for Disease Control and Prevention (website), accessed March 13, 2023, cdc.gov/violenceprevention/datasources/nisvs.

21 "Mental Health Matters," *The Lancet Global Health* 8, no. 11 E1352 (2020): https://www.thelancet.com/journals/langlo/article /PIIS2214-109X(20)30432-0/fulltext#articleInformation.

22 American Psychiatric Association, *Diagnostic and Statistical Manual of Mental Disorders: DSM-5* (Washington, DC: American Psychiatric Association, 2013).

23 "Prevalence of Any Mental Disorder Among Adolescents," National Institute of Mental Health (website), accessed March 13, 2023, nimh .nih.gov/health/statistics/mental-illness#part_2632.

24 Eunice Park-Lee et al., "Receipt of Services for Substance Use and Mental Health Issues among Adults: Results from the 2016 National Survey on Drug Use and Health," Substance Abuse and Mental Health Services Administration (website), published February 13, 2018, europepmc.org/article/NBK/nbk481724.

25 "Stigma, Prejudice and Discrimination Against People with Mental Illness," American Psychiatric Association (website), accessed March 20, 2023, psychiatry.org/patients-families/stigma-and -discrimination.

26 Tappert, *Luther*, 107.

27 For more information, see Tappert, *Luther*, 52.

28 Susan Mattern, "Galen and His Patients," *The Lancet* 378 (August 2011): 478–79, doi.org/10.1016/S0140-6736(11)61240-3.

29 Martin Luther, "Table Talk," Christian Classics Ethereal Library (website), 1566, § 593, https://www.ccel.org/ccel/luther /tabletalk.v.xxv.html.

30 Tappert, *Luther*, 17.

31 Luther, "Table Talk," § 600.

32 Tappert, *Luther*, 18.

33 Margaret A. Currie, *The Letters of Martin Luther: Selected and Translated by Margaret A. Currie* (London: MacMillan and Company, 1908), 72.

34 Currie, *The Letters of Martin Luther*, 343.

35 Currie, *The Letters of Martin Luther*, 211.

36 Currie, *The Letters of Martin Luther*, 212.

37 Currie, *The Letters of Martin Luther*, 79.

38 Luther, "Table Talk," § 739.

39 Tappert, *Luther*, 85.

40 Tappert, *Luther*, 93.

41 Currie, *The Letters of Martin Luther*, 218.

42 Tappert, *Luther*, 99.

43 *Luther's Correspondence and Other Contemporary Letters*, eds. Preserved Smith and Charles M. Jacobs, vol. 2, *1521–1530*. (Eugene, OR: Wipf and Stock), 409.

44 *Luther's Correspondence*, 2:409.

45 *Luther's Correspondence*, 2:408.

46 *Luther's Correspondence*, 2:408.

47 Currie, *The Letters of Martin Luther*, 65.

48 For more information, see E. Brooks Holifield, *A History of Pastoral Care in America: From Salvation to Self-Realization* (Eugene, OR: Wipf and Stock, 1983).

49 For more information, see Holifield, *A History of Pastoral Care*.

50 "Emmanuel Movement," Emmanuel Church in the City of Boston (website), accessed March 13, 2023, emmanuelboston.org/mission /history/emmanuel-movement/.

51 For more information, see John A. Bernau, "From Christ to Compassion: The Changing Language of Pastoral Care," *Journal for the Scientific Study of Religion* (February 2021).

52 Currie, *The Letters of Martin Luther*, 75.

53 Roland H. Bainton, *Here I Stand: A Life of Martin Luther* (New York: Abington Press, 1950), 42.

54 David Scaer, "The Concept of *Anfechtung* in Luther's Thought," *Concordia Theological Quarterly* 47 (1983): 15.

55 Martin Luther, *Luther's Works*, vol. 77, *Church Postil*, "Sermon for Easter Monday on Luke 24:13–35," eds. Benjamin T. G. Mayes and James L. Langebartels (St. Louis: Concordia Publishing House, 2014), 46.

56 Luther, *Luther's Works*, vol. 77, *Church Postil*, 47.

57 M. Vernon Begalke, "Luther's *Anfechtungen*: An Important Clue to His Pastoral Theology," *Consensus* 8, no. 1 (1982): 5, https://scholars.wlu.ca/consensus/vol8/iss3/1/.

58 Tappert, *Luther*, 87.

59 For more information, see Peter Preus, *And She Was a Christian: Why Do Believers Commit Suicide?* (St. Louis: Concordia Publishing House, 2011).

60 Luther, *Luther's Works*, vol. 77, *Church Postil*, "Sermon for Easter Tuesday on Luke 24:36–47," eds. Benjamin T. G. Mayes and James L. Langebartels (St. Louis: Concordia Publishing House, 2014), 86–87.

61 Robert D. Preus, "Clergy Mental Health and the Doctrine of Justification," LCMS, 2005, LCMS-Mercy-Booklet-Series-Clergy-Mental-Health-and-the-Doctrine-of-Justification.pdf.

62 Martin Luther, "Heidelberg Disputation (1518)," Book of Concord Online (website), accessed March 13, 2023, https://bookofconcord.org/other-resources/sources-and-context/heidelberg-disputation/.

63 Tappert, *Luther*, 87.

64 Tappert, *Luther*, 85.

65 Tappert, *Luther*, 98.

66 Tappert, *Luther*, 119.

67 Tappert, *Luther*, 121.

68 Luther, *Luther's Works*, vol. 34, *Careers of the Reformer IV*, ed. Lewis William Spitz, trans. Helmut T. Lehmann (St. Louis: Concordia Publishing House, 1960), 336–37.

69 Tappert, *Luther*, 124.

70 Tappert, *Luther*, 30.

71 Tappert, *Luther*, 105–8.

72 Tappert, *Luther*, 106.

73 Tappert, *Luther*, 107.

74 Tappert, *Luther*, 107.

75 Franzo Law II et al., "Vocabulary Size and Auditory Word Recognition in Preschool Children," *Applied Psycholinguistics*, National Library of Medicine (website), May, 11, 2016, https://www.ncbi.nlm.nih.gov /pmc/articles/PMC5400288/.

76 For more information, see Daniel Kahneman, *Thinking, Fast and Slow* (New York: Farrar, Straus and Giroux, 2013).

77 For more information, see Marcus Aurelius, *Meditations*.

78 Tappert, *Luther*, 102.

79 Tappert, *Luther*, 102–3.

80 Tappert, *Luther*, 92–93.

81 Tappert, *Luther*, 94.

82 Tappert, *Luther*, 94.

83 Tappert, *Luther*, 134.

84 Tappert, *Luther*, 85–86.

85 Tappert, *Luther*, 85.

86 Tappert, *Luther*, 117–18.

87 Tappert, *Luther*, 85.

88 Currie, *The Letters of Martin Luther*, 221.

89 Tappert, *Luther*, 96.

90 Tappert, *Luther*, 117.

91 Tappert, *Luther*, 85.

92 Tappert, *Luther*, 93.

93 Tappert, *Luther*, 84.

94 Tappert, *Luther*, 89–90.

95 *D. Martin Luthers Werke: Tischreden* (Weimar: H. Böhlau, 1912–21), § 3799.

96 Tappert, *Luther*, 97.

97 Tappert, *Luther*, 89.

98 Tappert, *Luther*, 85.

99 Tappert, *Luther*, 93.

100 Tappert, *Luther*, 93.

101 Tappert, *Luther*, 120.

102 Tappert, *Luther*, 95.

103 Tappert, *Luther*, 89–90.

104 Tappert, *Luther*, 97.

105 Currie, *The Letters of Martin Luther*, 212.

106 Tappert, *Luther*, 36.

107 Tappert, *Luther*, 92–93.

108 Bob Smietana, "Getting Beyond the Stigma of Mental Illness," Lifeway Research (blog), published November 11, 2014, https://research .lifeway.com/2014/11/11/getting-beyond-the-stigma-of-mental -illness/.

109 Robert D. Preus, "Clergy Mental Health and the Doctrine of Justification," LCMS, 2005, LCMS-Mercy-Booklet-Series-Clergy -Mental-Health-and-the-Doctrine-of-Justification.pdf.

110 Tappert, *Luther*, 46.

111 Tappert, *Luther*, 46–47.

112 For more information, see Rick Marrs, "Finding a Therapist," *Lutheran Witness* (2023): 22–23.

References

Anderson, Herbert. "Whatever Happened to *Seelsorge*?" *Word and World* 21, no. 1 (2001): 32–41.

Bainton, Roland H. *Here I Stand: A Life of Martin Luther.* New York: Abington Press, 1950.

Bernau, John A. "From Christ to Compassion: The Changing Language of Pastoral Care." *Journal for the Scientific Study of Religion* 60, no. 2 (2021): 362–81.

Clebsch, William A. and Charles R. Jaekle. *Pastoral Care in Historical Perspective.* New York: Harper and Row, 1964.

Currie, Margaret A. *The Letters of Martin Luther: Selected and Translated by Margaret A. Currie.* London: MacMillan and Company, 1908.

Holifield, E. Brooks. *A History of Pastoral Care in America: From Salvation to Self-Realization.* Nashville: Abingdon Press, 1983.

Kellerman, Bob. *Counseling Under the Cross: How Martin Luther Applied the Gospel to Daily Life.* Greensboro: New Growth Press, 2017.

Pless, John T. "Martin Luther: Preacher of the Cross." *Concordia Theological Quarterly* 51, nos. 2–3 (1987): 83–102.

Pless, John T. *Martin Luther: Preacher of the Cross.* St. Louis: Concordia Publishing House, 2013.

Preus, Robert. "Clergy Mental Health and the Doctrine of Justification." 2005, LCMS-Mercy-Booklet-Series-Clergy-Mental-Health-and-the-Doctrine-of-Justification.pdf.

Scaer, David. "The Concept of *Anfechtung* in Luther's Thought." *Concordia Theological Quarterly* 47, no. 1 (1983): 15–30.

Tappert, Theodore J., ed. and trans. *Luther: Letters of Spiritual Counsel.* Louisville: Westminster John Knox Press, 1955.